Looking For a Better Country

By
Helen Eickmann

TEACH Services, Inc.
Brushton, New York

Copyright © 1996 TEACH Services, Inc.

ISBN 1-57258-070-4
Library of Congress Catalog Card No. 95-62171

Published by

TEACH Services, Inc.
RR 1, Box 182
Brushton, New York 12916

Table of Contents

Acknowledgments

To Tamy Randolph and Edwin DeKock who helped me with my writing, and my husband, Peter, who also helped me with proofreading. Without his patience and encouragement during the years it took me to write, it would not have been possible to finish this little book. And with my prayers that my writings may be an encouragement for those who face difficult times, and help them to turn to their and my Saviour and best friend, Jesus.

Chapter 1

Germany

The sun gilded the banks of the river Elbe, the docks and ships at the pier in Hamburg, Germany. Helen held Peter's hand as they stood at the railing of the small freighter *Klaus Horn.* It was a September evening in 1938 and they were on their way to Haiti in the West Indies.

She heard the shrill cries of the seagulls overhead, the dull sound of the motor, and the rattle of the anchor chains. She felt the shudder of the ship under her feet, as it ever so slowly pulled away from the crowded piers. She waved as long as she could see the forms of her mother and Peter's father standing at the edge of the pier.

"We may be back in a year, Helen." Peter, her husband of ten days said.

There was a smile in his hazel eyes behind horn-rimmed glasses. The wind tousled his brown wavy hair, the same color as hers. He was only a few inches taller than her five and a half feet, but he seemed to have so much strength. She loved him. She felt secure with him.

"My contracts with my export firms are only for one year." He continued as he put his arm around her. "We'll see them again soon. You don't have to be sad."

Sad? She shook her head. She was not sad. Her heart almost burst for happiness. She felt like a bird released from its cage. She felt happy and free from the frustrations she had experienced lately.

These years in which Helen grew up had been difficult years for Germany. After the first world war ended unemployment was rampant. In 1933, when she was nineteen years old, the aged president, Paul von Hindenburg, had appointed Adolf Hitler as chancellor. The next year was election year.

It came after the worst inflation in Germany. Many German towns had printed their own money. It was called "Notgeld" (emergency money). Working people were paid twice a day. They went to buy food and other necessities at the stores as soon as they got paid. The money received at noon was worth much less in the evening. At the end of the inflation a Mark with twelve zeros was converted into one Goldmark.

There were only two parties able to win the Election: the Communists and the National Socialists. Helen did not want the Communists to take over Germany as they had Russia. The National Socialists with Hitler seemed to be the only hope. Helen, like many other people, did not at that

1

time understand the dark side of Hitler's party and where he would lead them.

The new party instituted many new projects. Work programs started to get the many unemployed young people off the streets. The boys and girls just out of school were required to work for a whole year either on farms or in households, for a small weekly allowance. Unemployment dropped, and after graduating from business college Helen was able to get a job as a typist with an attorney's firm.

The work week was six days. Helen loved to be out-of-doors and looked forward to the Sundays in summer when she could go hiking in the heather or the woods around Hamburg. One summer rain clouds gathered every weekend and on Sunday it rained. It was not possible to go hiking. It seemed to be a whole lost year.

Besides, shortly after Hitler came to power, a law was passed forbidding the transferring of currency out of Germany. The lawyer for whom Helen worked had cases where people were put in prison on *suspicion* they might try to send money to foreign countries. There were other cases she did not like. She became more and more unhappy with her job.

But it was through this job that her life took a different turn. A coworker asked one day, "Helen, would you like to go to a dance with my boyfriend and me? It's a nice place. I think you will like it."

"Thank you, Stephie," Helen said, "I'd love to."

It became a memorable evening. A young fellow not far from their table invited her to dance. He introduced himself as Hugo Eickmann. He danced the whole evening only with her. He sat down again when someone else was first in asking her for a dance. That impressed Helen. She did not refuse when he asked her for a date.

He told her he represented several manufacturers in Germany. Before that he had been assistant buyer in an export house for South America. He also spoke French, English, and Spanish.

Helen had good times with her new friend, boating on the Alster, watching the fireworks on Wednesday nights, and dancing. She fell in love with him.

The only thing she did not like was his given name. She just had seen the film of *A Man called Peter,* She liked the hero who portrayed a dedicated Christian, even if she did not believe in God. She asked Hugo if it would be all right to call him *Peter,* and he agreed.

It was the happiest time in Helen's life, but still there was a nagging fear of what was to come. There were ominous changes in Germany. Some of her father's old Jewish customers disappeared. No one seemed to know what had happened to them. There were other cases she did not like.

2

"Peter, I would like to leave Germany," Helen said one day. "Many of my relatives have gone to other countries. Some went to New York, others to Texas. One uncle went to London. They do not want my cousins to belong to the Hitler Youth, because my aunt is English. I could go to my uncle. I think he would give me a job."

"I would like to go to South America," Peter said.

"South America?! That would be great. They must have more sunshine there than here in Hamburg."

A few days later, rain clouds covered the sky and little drizzle fell, when Peter met Helen after work. As they walked through the busy streets, Helen saw a little grin on his face. She saw his face redden as he spoke.

"Helen, I found two export houses interested in sending me out as their representative on a commission basis, for Haiti and the Dominican republic, for six months each. They agreed to pay a travel allowance. It is not much, but I think it will be enough. Would you like to go with me?"

"Oh, Peter, how can I go with you?" Helen felt her face getting hot. "How can that be? We would have to be married if you want me to go with you."

"That's right, that's what I mean." He stopped walking. His eyes looked into Helen's. He smiled, took her hand, and said, "We would have to be married."

Happiness welled up in her as he put an arm around her. To go with Peter to South America! That was almost too good to be true. She never would have dreamed that!

"O, Peter!" was all she could say. She would have liked to kiss him, but that was just not done in Hamburg with so many people in the street.

"The travel allowance has to be stretched to cover the expenses for both of us," Peter continued. "We have to be very frugal, but we'll be together."

"Yes, I know about the money. All I'm able to take out of Germany are ten Marks, and that won't last long!" She laughed.

"There's something else," Peter's forehead wrinkled. "I have to advise my firms that I won't work for them any more and that I am taking over the representation of the export houses. They want me to leave soon."

"Then we won't have much time for preparations for the wedding," Helen said.

"That's right. We have to get our passports and then go to the consuls of Haiti and Santo Domingo, to get our visas and find out a little more about those countries."

When they visited the consul of Haiti a few days later, he said, "if you want to travel from Haiti to Santo Domingo, you need a car with higher road clearance than the German cars have. The road crosses a river. There are no bridges. A German car is too low and would never make it."

Peter sold his car and bought a used American-built Ford Convertible from the American Embassy. Summer clothes take little space. Helen was happy to be able to take her favorite books in her small trunk. The export firms shipped the samples in wooden crates on the same steamer, a little freighter.

The voyage was to take twenty-eight days until they would arrive in Port-au-Prince, the capital of Haiti. Helen felt her heart beat when she thought of that wonderful honeymoon!

They were married in the St. Johannis church. It was a small wedding. Only the closest friends and a few relatives attended. It seemed important to Helen to be married in the church, in spite of being an atheist.

Her parents had sent Helen to the children's worship hour on Sunday mornings at the Lutheran St. Johannis church. Helen also had attended the Girls' Bible Club of the church for many years. They had met at the community center and the children sewed and embroidered little fancy-work to help raise money for a new church bell. The old one had been used for ammunition during the war. But no one ever had talked about a relationship with Jesus or said something about loving the Lord and giving their hearts to Him. She did not believe in God anymore by the time she was *confirmed* in the Lutheran church.

Her science teacher had taught evolution. That had appealed more to her. She quit attending her religion classes at school. But that was many years ago.

Now came the day of their departure. The freighter, *Klaus Horn,* was to sail September 20th. Helen's father had to attend to his business and could not go along to say farewell at the docks. There was a lump in her throat as she hugged him and kissed him good-by.

"It's only for a year, Papa." She saw tears in his eyes. "A year goes fast."

Her mother and Peter's father accompanied them to the harbor. But when they arrived, Helen did not see any large ocean liner. There was only a small freighter anchored at the pier.

"Where is the ship, Peter?"

"That's it." Peter pointed to the little freighter. "See, it says *Klaus Horn* right on the side of it."

"That looks more like a ship to sail on the Elbe. Do you think it's big enough to cross the ocean?"

Peter laughed. "It's big enough! It's a freighter and does not have many passengers. But it has made the trip many times. Don't you worry. It's going to be all right."

"We'll be back in a year, Mutti." Helen turned to her mother, hugged and kissed her. "You can come and visit us when we are established. It will not take long."

She said good-by to Peter's father. With trepidation she went up the gangplank to the small ship. It was a long way to the water below. Then she stood with Peter, waving to their loved ones. She did not realize that they never would see them again.

Chapter 2

Journey to the Antilles

Helen waved as long as she could see their loved ones. At last they vanished in the distance. Then a steward came to show them their cabin. He made them climb down some steep ship ladders. It was difficult. Helen dangled her foot to find the next rung on the ladder. The rungs were far apart.

The sun was shining through the round porthole as they entered their cabin. A bunk bed, a wash basin, and a place to store their luggage were crammed into the small space.

Soon a gong sounded for supper. The white dining-room, with its round portholes was small. Round tables looked festive with long white table cloths, set for four with plates, glasses, and silverware. There were only thirty passengers. Helen nodded "Good Evening" as they were introduced to some of the passengers and to the captain.

It was late when they came back to the cabin. Grey light streamed through the portholes when she awoke. There was not much to see outside, only grey water and grey sky.

"Let's go on deck," Peter said. "We still have a little time before breakfast."

"All right, but I hope we'll have breakfast soon. I'm hungry!"

Climbing up the ladder was easier. It was cool and foggy outside. Rows of deck chairs lined the side of the main deck.

"The chairs are for rent, Helen." Peter said. "We can rent them when the days get warmer."

Helen saw two slender young men wrapped in light-colored raincoats standing against the railing. They seemed to be about twenty years of age.

"My name is Schneider." The dark-haired, dark-eyed young man extended his hand to them. The twinkle in his eyes revealed that he was full of fun. "This is my friend, Gerlach." He pointed to the one with blue eyes under a thatch of unruly light hair. "We are going to Ciudad Trujillo, the capital of the Dominican Republic."

Later they met Mrs. Gunter, a Belgian, tall, slim, and always very elegant, returning to her importer husband in Santo Domingo. Some couples returned to the Caribbean after bringing their teenage children to Germany for their education. Among them was the consul from Cap Haiti, Consul Weber, who left his children and his wife in Germany; so she could take care of the children while they went to school. There were

6

some Haitians and Dominicans. They all became well acquainted during the twenty-eight days of the voyage.

The ship stopped in Antwerp, Belgium, for several hours. The passengers went on land.

"Helen," Peter said, "there's a department store across the street. Let's go in and shop around."

"Look at these folding chairs!" Peter said as they came to a display of garden furniture. "They cost less then the rent for the chairs on the boat. I'll buy two, and we can take them with us."

Peter carried the lightweight deck chairs while they were looking at some other displays. At last it was time to go back to the ship.

Entering the Bay of Biscay, the trip got a little rougher. A fierce wind blew.

Helen climbed over the heavy anchor chains and stood on the forecastle after one of the worst storms passed. The wind blew her hair, stroking her ears, tugging on her dress. Fine spray misted her face and tasted salty in her mouth. She saw the reflection of the rainbow in the mist and heard the cries of the ever-present seagulls. She thought of Peter and happiness filled her heart! What more could life offer?!

The weather cleared and became warmer after the ship passed the Bay of Biscay. Helen and Peter spent their time visiting with the other passengers, and playing shuffleboard with Schneider and Gerlach.

One day Helen stood at her favorite place at the bow of the ship. Peter, appearing beside her, said, "I thought I'd find you here! Come with me. I want to show you something." He took her hand.

"What is it?"

"Dolphins! Come, you can't see them from here."

They climbed back, past the windlass, and looked over the railing. "Look, there they are!"

Helen saw dark forms gliding out of the water, jumping over the aqua clearness, gently returning into the water in effortless play. The dolphins! She stood with Peter to watch the dolphins for a long time until the sun dipped beyond the horizon in a broad path of fire. The dusk was short. The stars appeared, one after the other. Night fell, but not darkness. The moonless sky blazed with an abundance of stars.

"Peter, it's beautiful! I have never seen so many stars, and the Milky Way! So clear! So bright!"

She looked up at the stars. Their brilliance illuminated the deck of the ship. The waves reflected the silver light. Farther south the ocean glowed with iridescent light, outlining the playing forms of dolphins which became faithful companions of the ship.

They spoke about God. "I think that those stories about Jesus and the Bible are only fairy tales," Helen said, "something like the German and Greek mythology."

"Fairy tales? I believe in God. Don't you?" Peter asked.

"No, I don't." she replied. "You know that. I remember one of my girlfriends once took me to a revival meeting. I didn't believe anything that the speaker said. I told her what Karl Marx said, 'Religion is the opiate of the people.' I'm not a Communist. I like the church. I believe in the Golden Rule. We should help each other and not hurt anyone."

"That's right. But I am a Lutheran and do believe in God."

"All right. But do you ever go to church?"

"Well,—on Christmas and Easter, I often went with my father to Mass. He is Catholic, but my mother is Lutheran, and they brought me up Lutheran."

"I don't know many Christians who really live their belief." Helen shook her head. Sorry, I just can't believe in God.

"Well, I don't know, Helen. I do believe." They did not talk any more about this subject.

One day a faint smudge appeared on the horizon. Helen wondered if it could be a ship, but it looked different.

"Peter, isn't that land?"

The faint image became stronger and widened. At last there was no doubt about it—they were approaching land. It still took a while until they arrived at the harbor. Huge silver colored tanks, marked "Shell," dominated the hills around. They had arrived at Curacao.

There was a cooling breeze while the ship moved, but now the heat lunged at her as she went with Peter down the gangplank. Peter held her hand as she stepped on to land. The harbor smelled like fish, dust, and sweat.

They inspected the one-storied bazaars. There were no showcase windows, no windows at all! Large wooden double doors opened to the street, displaying the merchandise in the cavernous stores, with large fans whirling under the high ceilings.

"Look at that, Helen." Peter pointed at some orange-brown suitcases. "They are real leather! I could use them for my samples when I visit the customers. And look at the price. My, they are cheap!"

He purchased two, one a little smaller than the other. Then they looked at the display of shoes.

"See those sandals, Helen. I like them. They look so comfortable. Let's see if they have our sizes."

They tried the sandals on. The leather felt soft and pleasant, and Peter bought matching sandals for both of them.

The ship stopped at several islands, and it took a few more days to get to Santo Domingo. Helen stood with Peter and other passengers at the railing, listening to some strange sounds wafting through the air.

"Listen, Peter! What is that sound? It sounds almost like music."

The cheerful, rhythmic tones got more distinct. At last the ship came close enough to see the people on the wharf. Fifteen or more musicians in colorful dress, with large, ornate, wide-brimmed hats, played violins, cello, trumpets, and other instruments Helen bad never seen or heard before.

"Those are mariachis." Consul Weber informed them.

"But what are those instruments?" Helen asked pointing to some which looked like oval-shaped balls fastened to sticks.

"They are maracas. They make that crickety noise. And look, there's Mr. Gunter. Seems that he hired the musicians to welcome his wife."

Quite a few of their travel companions disembarked. Helen saw Schneider and Gerlach walk down the gangplank. They turned around, waving at them from the pier.

Mrs. Gunter shook their hands and said, "Promise to call me when you come to Ciudad Trujillo, so that we can get together."

Helen and Peter kept standing at the railing until their friends disappeared in the customs house, and the musicians left. The next stop was Port-au-Prince, their destination. Helen could scarcely wait to get to their new country.

Chapter 3

Haiti, September 1938

Haiti, Santo Domingo or Hispaniola, as it is called, is an island of the Greater Antilles in the West Indies. It has cliffed coastlines and steep mountain ranges. On the rainy south slopes mahogany trees grow in the large forests. There are sizable coffee plantations, cocoa, tobacco, bananas, mangos, coconut and royal Palms. Sugar cane grows on irrigated land.

The island is divided into two countries. Santo Domingo, or the Dominican Republic, is located on the east side. The old capital, destroyed by an earthquake, was rebuilt as per the instruction of the dictator Rafael Trujillo and named after him. It was *Ciudad Trujillo* during Helen and Peter's stay on the island. The population is mulatto, a mixture of Spanish, black, and Indians. The language is Spanish.

The Republic of Haiti, a more arid country, is located on the Western part of the island. The capital is Port-au-Prince, situated on the coast between high mountain ranges. Its temperature is among the hottest in the cities of the Antilles. The population is black. The language is French for the more affluent ones, many of them well educated in France, and Patois for the poorer classes.

Not many other countries have a history as tumultuous, full of violence and tragedy as Haiti. "Ahitj," as the Indians called it, was discovered by Columbus in 1492. The reef of Cap Haiti is supposed to hold the remains of the "Santa Maria," the flagship of Columbus.

Under foreign rule the eight hundred thousand, or possibly one million to three million Indians, were massacred, exploited, and worked to death in the rich gold mines until only a few were left. Buccaneers and pirates massacred the rest of them.

The French took over the island. The import of slaves from Africa began. Haiti flourished under the French rule. The yearly export to France mushroomed, but this was achieved only through mistreatment and exploitation.

At last the slaves revolted. One of them, Jean Jacques Dessalines, became president. He hated and killed all whites and anyone mixed with white blood. He declared that only blacks were allowed to live in Haiti. He tore the white out of the flag and left only the sky-blue and blood red. Irrigation projects decayed. Export ceased. The country's prosperity vanished.

After many new revolts, coups, and assassinations the United States intervened. But it took many more years to achieve a semblance of stability in the country. This was the situation during the time Helen and Peter spent their first six months together in this tortured land.

The ship arrived in the evening. The sun was a narrow orange slice on the horizon as they approached land. The windows of the custom house reflected the fading light. Darkness settled fast. There were no lights on the pier. Helen saw a few narrow boats approaching the ship. An officer told them that the ship was too large to get any closer to land.

"You have to climb down the rope ladder to the boats. They'll bring you to the pier," he said, opening a gate on the railing.

Helen bent over the railing. She felt her heart throbbing as she saw a long rope ladder hanging at the side of the ship reaching far down into the water. The first passengers stepped off the ship to descend to the narrow long boats, bobbing on the waves.

"Peter, I don't like this. Is there no other way to get to land?"

"I'm afraid not. Just hold on tightly."

Her heart beat wildly. She grabbed the heavy rope, turning her face toward the ship. Her foot dangled to find the next rung. The rungs were much farther apart than on the ladder in the ship! Slowly she descended, rung after rung.

At last she felt a hand reaching out, steadying her. She found a place to sit in the unsteady boat. Peter came right behind her. Some natives brought the suitcases and the folding chairs. A few people, most of them natives, stood on the pier, waiting to help the passengers.

Many of the remaining passengers on the ship continued their voyage to Cap Haiti. Friends and families picked up the few who lived near Port-au-Prince. Soon they disappeared. Helen and Peter stood alone on the pier with their hand baggage and deck chairs. It was getting dark. Helen could see only a few natives in the distance.

"What are we going to do, Peter? How can we get the car out of customs? How can we get to the city?" She looked around. Fear welled up in her. "There is nobody we can ask for directions! How do we find a hotel?"

Before Peter could answer, Helen saw a tall, slim gentleman hurrying toward them.

"Are you Mr. and Mrs. Eickmann?" He asked in German.

"Yes, we are," Peter said. "But how do you know about us?"

"My boss in Hamburg is a friend of the owners of your firm. He asked me to help you to find lodging. It is too late to find a place tonight. Customs are closed. I'll take you to my house and help you tomorrow to find a place to stay and get your things out of customs."

Helen took a deep breath. She felt a heavy weight being lifted from her. Things would work out all right! Their new friend led them to a car parked close by. They drove out of the harbor district, through the dark town, toward the hills. The car bounced and shook on the bumpy road, from one pothole to the next. Suddenly there was a crashing noise! The car stopped, sagging to one side. Their benefactor went out to investigate.

"An axle is broken," he groaned. "But at least we are close to my house. Let's take your things and walk the rest of the way. I will have the car towed and fixed tomorrow."

Helen did not worry any more; she was confident, tomorrow they would find a place to stay for the next six months. Their new benefactor would help them. They spent the first night in their new country in a lovely room. The future looked bright.

The next morning they took a taxi to the docks. It did not take long to go through customs. What a relief to have their own car again!

They drove through downtown Port-au-Prince. What a noisy bustle! Taxis honked. Busses screamed their "Yeehoo, Yeehoo!" Radios blared, and peddlers cried out their wares. Lofty arcades tried in vain to shelter the shops from the heat. The stores looked very much like the ones in Curacao, revealing behind their massive doors tables and shelves laden with merchandise in colorful array.

Helen saw mostly black people: some men dressed in neat white suits and ties, not in shirt-sleeves, in spite of the heat, others barefoot, in rags; women, walking straight as a rail, dressed in long, wide skirts, sashes around their waists, colored head-cloths setting off their dark faces, carrying bundles of clothes, baskets with fruit, and other loads on top of their heads! Some vendors squatted under the arcades with little stands before them offering their merchandise: oranges, grapefruits as large as a child's head, a variety of bananas, and fruits Helen did not recognize, and other strange-looking foods.

The road widened after they passed the business section of Port-au-Prince. Peter stopped the car and looked at the hand-drawn map he received in the morning.

"We have to pass the Champ-de-Mars. That's where the government buildings are, and the parade grounds. Beyond that is Petionville, the residential section, where the boarding house is."

It was still morning, but the heat already brooded over the large expanse of lawn while they drove over the Champ-de-Mars. White government buildings glistened in the distance.

The road narrowed going uphill to Petionville. Hibiscus and bougain-villas bloomed in profusion. Tropical vines, stately Royal Palms, and other plants sheltered the buildings. The homes looked like pictures of old hacienda mansions, with broad porticos, wide steps, and spacious verandas. They were built of wood, with wooden shutters.

The boarding house was located on the outskirts of Petionville. Peter and Helen mounted the wide steps. A sturdy native girl escorted them to a gentleman, medium size, stocky, with light-brown hair and blue eyes.

"My name is Keller," he said in German. "I'm the owner. I heard you were coming." He shook their hands.

He introduced them to his wife, petite, graceful, with just a little lighter skin than most Haitians.

"Come in!" he said, motioning them to enter.

A round table with a richly embroidered tablecloth hanging to the floor dominated the first room. Behind that came a larger room with a long table and chairs on all sides; then an open, roofed veranda.

The kitchen consisted of a little open shack without windows, separated from the house. The walled-in swimming pool looked promising. It took most of the backyard, which was ablaze with bright-red bougainvillea and hibiscus.

"Come," Mrs. Keller said, "I'll show you your room."

They climbed the wide wooden stairway to the bedrooms in the second story. An enormous mosquito net fastened to a wooden square at the ceiling enclosed an ample bed. There was plenty of room for the wardrobe, a small table and two chairs.

Helen liked the spaciousness of the room. She was glad when Mrs. Keller quoted a price which was within their means.

They met the other boarders at lunch: a middle-aged couple with two teenagers, and a single man. All the guests took their meals together on the veranda, while an oversized fan tried in vain to bring a little cooling.

The food did not taste as Helen thought it should. She looked forward to the chocolate pudding, but it tasted like vanilla, not like chocolate! The same happened to most of the other dishes, with the exception of the canned peaches, imported from the United States. How she wished she could have seconds! But there was only one half peach for each person.

It was hot! Helen looked at the thermometer beside the window. The mercury went to the top. She wondered why it did not break from the pressure. It was hot everywhere! There was no escaping from it. Not the smallest cloud marred the deep blueness of the sky.

The night did not bring relief. It got dark early. Helen looked out the open window of their room. She saw the palm trees across the street turned into pure silver from the light of the moon. The house, the plants in the yard, everything was shining in pure silver light. She heard the "tom-tom, tom-tom" of the drums during the night. Voodoo drums? She did not know.

Peter traveled a lot, visiting the importers in surrounding towns. Haiti was not a prosperous country. There was little industry. Many things had to be imported. Their samples consisted of enamel dishes, cheap silverware, kerosene cookers, hardware items, even canned fish. Besides these practical things, Peter had samples of beautiful silks from France, but he could get orders only for as much as was needed for one evening gown. The stores could sell each pattern to only one customer. Only the well-to-do could afford such luxuries, and it would have caused a scandal to have two ladies with the same material meet at one of the elegant functions of society.

Helen was glad that she had attended a business college. She did some office work, typing, and delivered telegrams to the customers. The days were busy, but there was an emptiness in her life which she could not explain.

Peter and Helen went dancing on Saturday nights until early in the morning, and Helen battled hangovers on Sundays. But no matter how late they returned, they did not have any problems waking up. Early in the morning, Chee-Chee, the little black girl, handed each of them a small demitasse of very strong, very sweet coffee, with a peculiar burned taste. From the street sounded the "clonk, clonk, clonk" of the shoeshine boys, hitting their wooden boxes with short clubs, yelling for their customers with shrill voices.

Christmas came. It did not seem like Christmas. It was hot, the sunshine too bright! There was no Christmas music, no frost in the air, no Christmas decorations. Helen and Peter went to Midnight Mass at the large cathedral in town. The church was packed with ladies dressed in elegant gowns, well-groomed men and people in rags. Helen was disappointed that she could not understand anything the priest said.

Peter and Helen went on outings with their new acquaintances. One time Helen stepped on a thorn. The thorn came through the sole of her shoe, piercing her foot. Her foot swelled to over double its size. Peter left the next morning. Helen showed her foot to Mrs. Keller. Mrs. Keller handed her a small jar. "Here is some Vicks ointment, Madame Eickmann," she said, "Put that on your foot. It will help to get the swelling down."

Helen bandaged her foot as well as she could. Then a telegram arrived that had to be delivered to one of the customers. The telegram was important. They could not afford to lose any orders. How could she get down to Port-au-Prince? It did not occur to her to take a taxi. That was not in their budget.

Helen wore the new sandals from Curacao most of the time. But there was no way to get her swollen foot into it now. She looked around the room to see what she could put on the swollen foot. Her glance fell on Peter's sandals. How fortunate, she thought, that they got the shoes in Curacao. She was just able to squeeze her foot into one of them. It hurt when she stepped on it, but she could hobble down to Port-au-Prince and deliver the telegram with a perfectly matching pair of shoes, one size 7½, the other man's size 9.

Helen got her first taste of tropical lightning storms when the rainy season started. She did not see any raindrops. The rain came down like roaring waterfalls. Then came blinding lightning after lightning. The thunder boomed to split her ears. The storms did not last long. The sun blazed again. The heat got more oppressive with the new moisture in the air. Helen was glad when their six months in Haiti were over and it was time to move to another country, Santo Domingo.

Chapter 4

Rags and Riches

Peter planned to visit his customers in Aux-Cayes on their way to Santo Domingo. Because the United States Navy was on maneuvers in Aux-Cayes, it was difficult to get a room in a hotel.

At last Peter found a place to stay overnight. The owner of the hotel warned them not to carry any money with them, because all the pickpockets of the island were assembling at the city. Peter had saved a little over two hundred fifty dollars during the six months in Port-au-Prince.

"Helen, I'm afraid to keep the money with me," he said. "We cannot afford to lose it. It will be another month before we get another travel allowance."

"Where do you want to keep it then?"

"I don't know where there is a safe place. Maybe we should put it in the car."

The next morning they went to the car to continue their journey. Peter, keys in hand, looked at the top of the car.

Helen saw his mouth fall open. He clutched his hand to his breast. "Helen," he shouted, "someone has opened the cover at the side!"

Peter opened the glove compartment. His horror-stricken face told Helen the grim news: the money was gone!

"What are we going to do?" he said, choking out the words.

She did not know. She was in shock herself.

"It'll take almost a month until we get another travel allowance." Peter shook his head. "We have barely enough money to get through the next few days. We have to buy gas to make it to Ciudad Trujillo and to get around there. We have to stay in the cheapest places the next couple of nights."

"And we have to get something to eat!"

"Helen," Peter said after a stunned silence, "our next stop is Cap Haiti. Consul Weber asked us to visit him when we come his way. He gave me his address. Maybe he'll ask us to stay overnight. We have to be very careful in what we spend."

Consul Weber welcomed them with outstretched hands, his face creased in smiles. "It's good to see some countrymen again!" he said.

Helen was glad to hear him say: "Hope you can stay overnight! It gets lonely in this big house." He gave a short laugh.

They got up at daybreak, having breakfast on the terrace overlooking the ocean. Helen saw the large, red sun rise out of the ocean. The waves reflected the ever-widening path of light until the sun separated from the horizon.

They talked about many things. It was obvious that consul Weber enjoyed talking with someone in his native language. Then the talk turned to the conditions of the road leading to Santo Domingo.

"You know that a river marks the border between the two countries," said the consul, "and there is no bridge. You will have to drive through the river. Try to get over the middle of it. When you get stuck before the middle, people from Haiti have to push you over the middle. Then the Dominicans have to push you the rest of the way unto land. You would have to pay twice. But if you can make it over the middle, you pay only once.

"We haven't had much rain. Maybe you will be lucky. Remember to turn to the left in the river. The road goes up the bank, a little to the left."

Peter did not tell the consul anything about their financial crisis. After leaving the consul, he bought oranges and bananas for their next meals. Enclosed in their peels, they seemed to be the safest food. Then they continued their journey.

It was evening when Helen and Peter got to the river marking the border. The large orb of the sun touched the horizon, then slowly sank out of sight.

"We have to hurry, Peter, to get through the river before it gets dark!"

Peter steered the green Ford convertible slowly down the slope leading to the river. Helen scanned the other side to find the road leading out of the water, but the high trees and shrubs growing on the other side hid any exit.

Peter stopped for a moment before he stepped on the accelerator. The car splashed into the water. The waves came over the running board. He steered the car slowly toward the middle of the stream. Helen looked to see if there was anyone to help them if they got stuck. In the gathering darkness there was not a soul in sight. Her heart started to beat wildly.

"We made it to the middle! Now we only have to get out of this river, and up the bank." Peter sounded cheerful.

"What if we get stuck and there is nobody around to help us?" Helen did not share Peter's enthusiasm. "Can you see where we can drive up?"

"No, not yet."

Peter continued slowly steering closer to the bank. At last she saw a spot where the shrubs seemed to stand a little farther apart.

"Peter, do you think this could be the road?"

"Let's try it. The ends of the road should not be so far apart. The consul would have told us. He said only to steer to the left."

Slowly Peter drove up the incline. "It's the road! We were lucky that we didn't get stuck!"

"Look, there is a light." Helen said, pointing to a small speck of light ahead, faintly illuminating the darkness. Peter drove toward it. It turned out to be a small hotel.

They entered through a creaking door. The inside walls, once white, needed paint. Large dirty sheets instead of walls separated the different rooms, but the stocky, black-haired attendant greeted them with a warm smile, his dark eyes exuding kindness and goodwill. He quoted a ridiculously low price. There did not seem to be another hotel nearby. Peter checked in.

"Peter, what are these little black things?" Helen examined the almost white linen. "I never saw anything like this."

"I don't know," was his answer.

She figured that this was their introduction to bedbugs. She felt exhausted. They tried to pick the bedbugs off their bed, and to get comfortable on the lumpy mattress. Then, listening to Peter's even breathing, she fell asleep at last.

They continued their trip as soon as the sun rose in the morning. Short, scrubby brush flanked the dusty, winding road.

"I'll see if we can make this hill to save on gas," Peter said. He accelerated at the bottom of the hill, then coasted down, trying to get as high as possible on the next one.

For meals they had their bananas and oranges. Peter did all right on that diet. The longer Helen ate those fruits, the hungrier she got. At last, it felt only like a swallow of water without anything solid in it. She was hungry!

They made it all right to Ciuded Trujillo. What a contrast to Port-au-Prince! Modern buildings with large display windows, made out of glass instead of wooden shutters! Clean sidewalks in good repair! The people looked more prosperous. Only the traffic was about the same—the one who honked loudest went first.

They found an inexpensive but clean little boarding house. After they moved in, Peter said, "I'm going to call Mrs. Gunter. Remember, she asked us to call her when we got here."

"Mrs. Gunter invited us for tea tomorrow," he said when he came back. "She gave me the directions to get to her house."

The next afternoon they drove through a neighborhood with wide streets, flanked by palm trees, with expensive, modern, flat-roofed, homes.

"There, that is the house," Peter said, pointing to a one-story white building.

The house was surrounded by trumpet vines, bougainvilleas and hibiscus. They climbed the few steps to an open veranda. A black man in a white linen suit answered their knock at the door, leading them into a spacious living-room. Two enormous German shepherd dogs lay spread-eagled on the polished tile floor. An immense comfortable-looking sofa half surrounded a coffee table. They saw a large dining table with chairs and a beautiful sideboard in the adjacent room, and beyond another open veranda with a view of the trees and shrubs of the back yard.

"How nice that you called me right away!" Mrs. Gunter shook their hands.

She looked just as Helen remembered her from the steamer, tall and slim, with beautifully coifed hair, in a long, red and yellow flowered, silky dress. She motioned them to sit in the cozy corner. The man in white, the butler, served iced tea and delicious pastry.

Their hostess showed them the rest of the house, introducing them to the cook, Rebecca, who resembled the women in Haiti. She was dressed in a native wide skirt and blouse, looking very clean. She was from Trinidad and spoke English like the butler.

"You know," Mrs. Gunter said, her head bent to the side, looking at Peter after a short conversation. "My husband and I want to go to New York for three months. Would you know someone who would be interested in renting our house for that time?"

"They could pay the rent after we come back," she said after a little while, interrupting the stunned silence.

Helen scarcely believed her ears. Did Mrs. Gunter suggest that they should rent the house? She must know that they could not know anyone here in Santo Domingo. But living in a house like this?! She would never have thought of it!

She heard Peter's voice, "We may be interested, but how much is the rent?"

Mrs. Gunter quoted a low price and said, "The servants get fifteen cents a day for food and salary."

Helen looked at Peter. He accepted the offer, her own big smile reflecting in his face.

"What are we going to do about money to buy food and to pay the servants?" Helen asked on the way back to the boarding house.

"I don't know, Helen. The only thing I can think of is to call Schneider and Gerlach, whom we met on the ship coming over. They are working for the German Embassy. There are three rooms one could use as bedrooms. Maybe we should ask them if they would like to live with us for these three months. And they probably won't even mind paying something in advance when we tell them our story. I really don't know what else to do. We are running out of money fast and there are still over three weeks until we get the next travel allowance."

Peter was right. The two young men accepted the proposal enthusiastically, and in a few days they together with Helen and Peter moved into that gorgeous house.

How their circumstances had changed dramatically in just a few days! In her wildest dreams Helen would never have thought that she would live in such a gorgeous house, having a cook, a butler, a washerwoman, and two enormous German shepherd dogs! How she enjoyed the three months in those beautiful surroundings, with some friends who spoke German! She did not even have to grope for words in French, let alone Spanish! It did not occur to her that God was leading them and cared for them.

Chapter 5

Santo Domingo

The three months in the beautiful home of the Gunter's passed only too fast. Afterwards Peter and Helen rented a small two-room apartment on the third floor of a building at the corner of Isabel La Catolica and Plaza Colon.

For the first time Helen had her own kitchen. Her stove consisted of two sunken squares for burning charcoal, set into a cement counter. The apartment had real glass windows with little panels. The glass panels seemed to be set in the wrong way, as the two rooms flooded every time a tropical storm came. But it was easy to wipe up the water from the colorful tile floor. Best of all was the view of the Plaza and the cathedral, and—beyond that,—the ocean. In the darkness of the night Helen could see the lights from the pier stretching a longing arm far out into the ocean to distant unknown shores.

Sometimes Helen went with Peter for a walk, looking in the windows of the stores at the Plaza Colon when the heat lessened a little in the evening. She especially liked one display of watches from a little jewelry store. The many kinds of watches, with so many multicolored dials, fascinated her. Peter's father was a watchmaker. Helen remembered his little shop as she was looking at the display.

"You know," Peter said, "I'd like to get a presentation of a Swiss watch factory. I bet, I can sell some watches here."

They continued their walk along the sea wall. Helen enjoyed the sound of the waves lapping at the narrow beach. The low-built houses on the land side looked as though they had been painted with a child's crayon set, with greens and pinks, and many other colors. Radios blared their love songs. Almost all songs ended with "mi corazon" (my heart).

It was a balmy tropical night at the beginning of September, 1939, when Peter and Helen went down to the Plaza. The light of the lanterns blotted out the brilliance of the stars overhead. The yellow glow illuminated the stone benches, the pavilion, the tropical shrubs, and palm trees. The cathedral of Isabel La Catolica was a dim silhouette in the background.

Every Thursday and Sunday night the military band marched in grand style to the Plaza to play. The band major looked like a giant toy soldier right out of the Nutcracker Suite in his fancy uniform, flaunting his baton in rhythm with the music.

They watched the young girls attired in their finery, walking around the pavilion in the center. The girls walked around in one direction, - the young men in the opposite, watching one another. Fragments of their comments drifted to her ears. The band played lively marches. One of her favorites was the National Anthem of Santo Domingo, by Souza.

They often met with Schneider and Gerlach, and another young man from the German embassy, Hendrich. This evening, September 2, 1939, Hendrich was sitting alone.

"Hi, what's new? Sit down." Hendrich's hand motioned to the empty place on the bench.

"Did you hear the news, Hendrich? There will be war." Peter sat down next to him.

A frown crossed Hendrich's handsome face. "There will be no war, Eickmann. What gave you that idea?"

"Mark my words. I'm telling you, there will be war. France and England will declare war. They will not be standing idly by while Hitler enters country after country."

Peter's eyes looked serious. He leaned forward, his shoulders hunched, his suntanned face turning to his friend as he tried to convince him of his opinion of impending doom. The argument went back and forth until it was quite late, but Hendrich did not agree with Peter.

Helen woke up with sunshine streaming into the windows of their apartment. She heard shouting from the street.

"Inglaterra y Francia han declarado guerra contra Alemania!" the paper boy bellowed.

"Helen, did you hear that? England and France have declared war against Germany!"

So, Peter had been right. She wondered what changes this would bring to their lives now. She did not have long to wait. Hitler had made a law that no money could leave Germany. Merchandise had to be exchanged in equal amounts between Germany and the exporting country. Because of this, Peter did not get any commissions remitted to him during the year, but had to order merchandise from his firms for the amount of his commissions. He had placed a large order of toys for the whole year's work, and they were now on a ship close to Curacao.

Shortly after that Peter came home with a heavy parcel.

"A package for you, Helen!"

It was from friends of her parents, from Germany. Eagerly she tore open the wrapping. On top was a cook book. The name, translated into English, was *Basic Recipes for the Culinary Arts.* Underneath was a scale, white, a foot long, eight inches wide, and five inches high, with chromed sliding weights, and a gleaming chrome tray on top.

22

"Oh, Peter, what a beautiful kitchen scale! But how in the world will I ever use it? I cannot cook much on the charcoal fires in the kitchen, and I don't have an oven. But it surely is beautiful!"

She heard Peter coming slowly up the stairs a few days after that. With a sigh he sat at the small table, stroking his chin.

"Helen," he said, "it seems the news is bad. The toys were confiscated in Curacao, and we will not get anything from my whole year's work."

"Oh, what are we going to do?"

"You know that our contracts with our firms are only for one year, and that year is about up. I don't think that we can go back to Germany now, and I don't think we will be able to do any business with Germany for some time to come." He shook his head.

"I doubt that I can get a job here. I think,—I really think the best would be if we would go to a larger country. Maybe there will be more opportunity for us to make a living."

"But where do you think we should go?"

"A few days ago I spoke with Schneider, and he wants to go to Caracas, Venezuela. I thought about going either to Colombia or Venezuela. Both countries are not so far. But I think Venezuela would be better. The trip is shorter and it will cost less."

"How much will it cost? How will we pay for the tickets? We don't have much money."

"I don't know how much the tickets are. The only way to pay for them is to sell the car."

He looked at her and sighed. "And that's not the only bad news. The steamship company told me I should not try to go by boat. The Allies are taking the German men off the ships as prisoners of war, when the ships dock at a harbor belonging to them. You will have to take the boat and all our belongings as passenger goods, and I will have to take the plane to Venezuela."

"You mean, I have to go to Venezuela alone?"

Helen stared at her husband. He had been her source of strength. He had such energy, always knew a way out, and worked hard. She felt secure with him. How could he think of letting her go alone?

"Don't worry, Helen. I'll leave early enough in order to meet you when the ship arrives at La Guaira, the port of Venezuela. The planes go only to Maiquetia, where the airport is. There will be a bus or something to get to La Guaira."

"Oh, Peter, I don't like that! I don't want to go alone! Can't we go together on the plane?"

He shook his head. "I'll be there. Don't worry. Besides you have to take all our things, the furniture, samples, everything, as passenger goods."

"You mean, they'll let me take all that on the boat?"

"Yes, and it will be much cheaper than trying to sell everything and buying new things."

"I can see that!"

Helen looked around their little two-room apartment. They could not afford any large expenditures. Fortunately all their sample collections came in large wooden boxes, ideal for making side tables and shelves. Peter had been quite handy in their construction, and after she had done the painting, they looked quite presentable, she thought. The wood was a little rough, but brown paint did wonders to it!

They had a bed made—just a rough frame, covered with some metal spirals to hold a thin mattress. The sides could be taken off and the bed rolled together. They had a little table, serving as desk and dining table, four chairs, the folding chairs they had bought at Antwerp, and a small wardrobe.

Kitchen utensils and appliances were no problem. She did not have many pots and pans, and only the barest supply of dishes and silverware, and her beautiful kitchen scale! No need for an icebox or a refrigerator! Anything left over could be brought to a boil and would keep another half day, to be used at the next meal.

The charcoal she burned for cooking presented a problem. After getting used to habitual smoke inhalation, she was not quite sure if that caused her sick feeling, or if there was some other reason. It did not take long to find out that she was expecting a baby.

The doctor said, "You have uremic poisoning and should not eat any kind of meat, eggs, fish, or chicken."

"But what can I eat instead?"

"Well, you can eat platanus, or plantain: you know the large cooking banana, which you can prepare in different ways, fried or boiled, mashed with onions on top. They are quite palatable, and have a lot of protein."

Helen did not ask anything more about the uremic poisoning, and the doctor did not volunteer any more information. She did not worry about it as long as she did not know what it meant. The doctor gave her the name of an English-speaking physician in Caracas before they left for Venezuela.

The time of their departure approached. Peter tried to sell his car and as many of his samples as he could.

"Helen," Peter said, "I can't find a buyer for the car. I'm afraid we have to drive back to Port-au-Prince. I know there are people who were interested in buying it."

They made the trip back to Haiti a few days later. Peter was right; he found a buyer right away. The new owner paid in "Gourds," Haiti's currency. Most of the money was printed in one and five Gourd bills. It took many bank notes to make up the amount for the car. The buyer wrapped the bills in newspaper. It made a package of a foot and a half square, six inches high. Peter took the heavy package under his arm to bring it to the bank to exchange it for dollars.

"I'm glad that went fast." Peter sighed. "The ship is sailing in a few days, and we have to do the packing still."

They took a bus back to Santo Domingo. Then Peter went to say good-by to his customers. Helen knew by the way he mounted the stairs that he had some good news. His face was one big smile when be spoke.

"Helen, one of my customers gave me twelve big barrels of honey for my commission for the last order, which had not yet been paid. I made arrangements to have them shipped to New York. Isn't that great? You know, I'm surely glad, because after paying for the tickets we only have about $ 90.00 left."

"Only $ 90.00? How can we live on that?"

"Don't you worry. We'll have the money from the honey too, and I'll get a job. Let's start packing."

Helen felt reassured. Peter knew what he was doing. He was right. She did not have to worry.

"I'm glad that we bought the two large suitcases in Curacao. You can take them as passenger goods," Peter said. "They hold a lot of the samples, even the two kerosene cookers, and everything we really need. Helen, you can also take the folding chairs with you. They are not too bulky."

"Now, let's hurry. Schneider promised to come by with a handcart to help us."

It was only a short distance to the little freighter anchored at the pier. Peter got her settled in her cabin.

"See you in La Guaira, Helen, and don't you worry, I'll be there." With a quick kiss be vanished.

Helen stood at the railing a minute later. Her gaze fastened on the corner of the street from where Peter and Schneider had to come. To her horror she felt a shudder of the ship. The engines started! She saw the heavy ropes being untied at the pier, heard the clanking of the chains lifting the anchor, and then felt the movement of the ship! The distance between the pier and the ship widened ever so slowly and there two men appeared around the corner with a handcart, piled high with a strange assortment of things. They came closer,—and all she could do was wave! The boat pulled out.

Helen was alone without their belongings on her way to Venezuela.

Chapter 6

Venezuela

Venezuela, situated just north of the equator, is the sixth largest country of South America. The Andes, a high mountain range, extends from Cape Horn, the southern end of Chile, all the way through South America to Venezuela's Caribbean coast at the north. At the east of the country the waters of the Angel Falls in La Gran Sabana (the Great Plain) plunge over 3,200 feet down. It is many times higher than the Niagara Falls! It got its name from an American pilot, Jim Angel, who saw the falls when he flew over it in his small private plane.

Venezuela is a rich country with gold mines, iron ore, copper, and oil. There are sugar cane, cocoa, and coffee plantations. There are many islands off the coast of Venezuela. The largest of them, Margarita, is known for its abundance of pearls.

Much of the south country is covered with tropical rain forests. A wide variety of orchids grow in the hot and moist atmosphere. There are many kinds of palm trees. In the highlands grow mangos, cashews, avocados, and many different kinds of bananas, from a small reddish banana and the "cambur manzana" (apple banana) to the large plantain. Breadfruit, guavas, and many other tropical fruits grow in the fertile soil. In the lowlands with its harsh climates are immense plains with large gnarled cacti and wild grasses, where hardy ranchers raise vast herds of cattle.

The climate varies widely. The temperature is cold in the high mountain ranges, spring-like in the low plains, and one of the hottest in South America at Maracaibo, situated on lake Maracaibo, off the Caribbean at the north end of Venezuela.

Simon Bolivar, "el libertador" (the deliverer), was the most famous of Venezuela's presidents. He won freedom from the Spaniards in 1821, and his statue adorns the plazas of Venezuela and Colombia.

It took five long days until the little freighter on which Helen was traveling got to Venezuela. She had some difficulties with the diet. The only food which her doctor allowed was sweet condensed milk and light, white French bread with butter.

There were few passengers on the small freighter, which was much smaller than the *Klaus Horn*. No one could speak English. Helen tried to converse with an Italian woman, plump and middle-aged, who sometimes occupied the deck chair at her side. The woman's dark eyes smiled encouragingly at her, but the few Spanish words Helen had picked up in

Ciudad Trujillo, interspersed with some French, did not lend themselves to lively conversation. She was alone most of the time, either in her small cabin or in a lounge chair on deck.

Many thoughts went through her mind. She wondered about their future. Life seemed so uncertain. How would they find jobs? How could they live on so little money? How would they find a place to live? Would Peter really be at the harbor when the ship arrived? What would she do if he was not there? How could she talk with the people? They did not understand English! Whom could she ask for help? She did not know anyone in Venezuela! Fear engulfed her. There was no answer for any of these questions.

She never thought of turning to God, for she did not believe that there was a God. But later she realized that He was watching over them and led them all along. But at that time the only thing certain in her life seemed to be that the baby was coming. She looked forward to it despite everything!

At last a smudge appeared on the horizon as the ship approached the harbor of La Guaira. A high, verdant mountain range stretched behind the dwellings and warehouses of the port on a narrow, palm-lined beach. Mount Avila loomed high in the distance.

As the steamer got closer to the shore, Helen anxiously scanned the people on the wharf, but could not see Peter. The ship docked, but she still did not see him. Cold claws of fear clutched her heart as she followed the other passengers down the ramp to the large custom building at the beginning of the pier. What would she do if he was not there? How would she find him if he missed his plane? What if something had happened to him, and she never would see him again? What would she do? And Peter was nowhere in sight.

She looked around to see if she could find someone who looked as if he could understand English, but she saw only some of the passengers and the native customs officials in their uniforms. She got through customs without having to say much. Numbly she followed the other passengers to the exit door. Her panic heightened, her heart beat wildly and there—right at the other side of the door—stood Peter!

"I was not allowed into the building. Hope you did not worry."

"Oh, Peter!" she threw her arms around him. "Am I glad you are here!"

"I told you so. I told you I would be here when the ship arrived."

"Yes, but…." She shook her head and sighed.

Then a thought struck her. "What about the furniture?"

"Schneider is coming in a few weeks. He promised to bring them with him."

Helen felt a large weight rolling off her heart. She smiled. Peter had found a solution. They had only to get to Caracas, and in a few weeks everything would be all right again. Just so she was with Peter. He would take care of everything.

The distance to Caracas, the capital of Venezuela, was only six or seven miles as the crow flies. But winding hairpin curves, twenty-five miles long, led up the mountain to the city at the time Peter and Helen traveled that road. Helen had just recuperated from the effects of one curve when they came to the next one. At last they got to the city! It took her three days for the earth to feel firm again.

Caracas spreads out in a long valley over 3,000 feet high on the base of mount Avila. Much has changed in Caracas during recent years. It is becoming a modern city with wide roads and skyscrapers, and even street names. But there were almost no street names when Peter and Helen arrived. The city was built in checkerboard form. The corners of the blocks had names. To give an address one had to give the names of the two corners of the block where the house was located, and the house number. They had strange names, like Carcel a Pilita (Prison to Small Stone), Corazon de Jesus a Coliseum (Heart of Jesus to Coliseum), Gradillas a Sociedad (Small Stepladder to Society), Pajaro a Zamuro (Bird to Vulture). Others were named after famous people.

Honking cars, yeehooing buses, donkeys laden with heavy loads filled the streets. Helen saw horse-drawn carts of the "fruteros," selling fruits and vegetables, and peddlers with large baskets, filled with a variety of objects; well dressed and poorly dressed men and women, school children in neat uniforms. The girls wore white blouses and dark blue skirts, the boys white shirts and dark pants.

They spent the first night in a cheap little hotel. The next morning Peter bought a newspaper.

"We have to see that we get something really cheap to live in, and make our money go as far as we can," he said.

He sat on the edge of the bed, opening the paper, looking for the advertisements. He started to read.

"This may be the right place. It cannot cost much." Peter put down the paper and looked at Helen. "It's just an unfurnished room, and it's close to the center of town."

"But.... but...where will we sleep? How can we live in an empty room?"

"We have the folding chairs. We can sleep in them."

"But we don't have money to go to a restaurant to eat. I'll need a kitchen. I have to do the cooking, and we need some chairs and a table."

"We have less than $ 90.00 left. I hope that we get the money from the honey, and that I get a job soon. But in the meantime we just have to get by the best we can. We will have to sit on a suitcase and use the other one as a table. We have the two kerosene stoves. We don't need them as samples anymore, and you can use them to cook on. It won't be forever. Schneider has promised to come soon, and he will bring our furniture."

They found the advertised room in a one-story house, built—like most of the houses—of stucco, with fancy wrought-iron bars protecting the windows of the recibo (the parlor) on the street side. A large wooden door led through a short hallway, which ran the width of the parlor. The door at the other end opened into the patio with colorful tile floors, alive with flowering plants. Statues adorned an elaborate water fountain. Both doors of the hallway were locked in the evening.

The doors and wooden-shuttered windows of the bedrooms lined one side of the patio. A wall divided the patio from the neighbor's house on the other side. Beyond the patio came the open, roofed dining room, and beyond that the kitchen and the bathroom, and a little yard at the end.

The middle-aged landladies looked very proper in long-sleeved, high-buttoned blouses and dark skirts. Their straight black hair was pinned up in a neat bun on top of their heads.

They showed them a room off the patio, with white painted walls, tile floor, and a wide window with an ample wooden sill. A lonely electric bulb dangled from its meager cord. The rent was cheap. They moved in with their suitcases and the two deck chairs.

How good that Helen brought their pillows and linen with her on the steamer! She liked the temperature of the much cooler climate.

They doubled the thin cotton blankets to get warm. Peter slept fine in his chair. Helen tried too, but could not get to sleep; only her arms did. They tingled and ached. There was no way she could stay in the chair all night. Where could she sleep? The tile floor was too hard and cold. She looked at the leather suitcases. One was a little higher than the other, but they felt much softer and warmer than the floor. Helen placed them end to end. They made an almost comfortable bed.

Peter left every day early in the morning to find a job, but without success.

"The money for the honey ought to come soon," he said, shaking his bead. "Our money is going to run out if we don't find a source of income soon."

Chapter 7

A Job!

The days in Venezuela do not change much in length during summer or winter. The longest day was only about an hour longer than the shortest. Darkness falls fast after the sun sets. Peter came home one evening at dusk, looking discouraged.

"Helen," he said, "I didn't find anything again today. What shall we do? Maybe we can make something I can sell?"

Helen rummaged through the suitcases. She held up the colorful silk samples from France. "Maybe I can make some evening purses out of these," she said.

It did not take long to sew a few small purses by hand, Peter took them the next morning, but came back with them, shaking his head.

"Helen, I could not sell the purses. There is no interest in them. What else could we manufacture that would sell?"

The silk samples were too small to make anything else, but at last a thought struck Helen. "Neckties are made of silk! They should not be too difficult to make and don't need very much material."

Helen took one of Peter's neckties apart to measure how much material she needed for a few neckties. Then they went to the yardage store.

"Look, Peter, this striped blue silk would look good for a tie, and this red one with a small pattern. What do you think?"

Peter approved her choices. He spent some of their fast diminishing wealth on the pretty patterned silk.

To save on material, Helen did not cut the neckties with the grain in her pattern. Maybe that was the reason that her creations curled like snakes. They would not lie flat. They did not sell.

"Peter," Helen asked. She looked worried. "What can we do to have some income?"

"We have to think of something soon, the money is running out fast," was Peter's not very reassuring answer.

At least they were able to have a good meal at noon. Peter discovered a German restaurant owned by Mr. Sittel. On the menu for lunch was bean, potato or lentil soup, as much as one could eat, for one real (fifty Bolivar cents) per person, about fifteen U.S. cents. They filled up on soup every noon. The other meals consisted of bread with butter and fruit. Margarine was not quite as satisfying, and Helen thought the butter would provide more nourishment for them and the baby. One good thing came out of her Spartan diet. She felt much better and did not have so much nausea.

At last the check for the honey arrived. Peter opened the envelope and took out the check. His eyes opened wide. He held the check in his hand, stared at it and did not say a word.

"How much is it? Tell me, how much is it?"

"Six Dollars! Only six Dollars."

He read aloud the accompanying letter. It said the seller was sorry he could not get more for the honey. The honey from Puerto Rico came into the United States duty free, while they had to pay duty on the honey from the Dominican Republic.

Peter tried again and again, but could not find a job. He sat on his suitcase a few days later, chin in hand. Then he looked up.

"Helen," he said, "if we could make something people eat or use up, something they would always need again, something like shoe creme, or something else they'd use every day, I think that would sell, but what?"

Helen thought of her fancy cookbook, *Basic Recipes for Culinary Arts*. She got it and opened it to the last pages.

"Look, Peter," She showed him the recipes for marzipan, the almond confection people use a lot for Christmas in Germany, and chocolates. "Maybe I can make some marzipan and chocolates."

"And Christmas is coming soon," Peter replied. "Remember, Mr. Sittel told us about a German club. I'm sure I could sell marzipan there."

"We even have the scale to measure the ingredients and the two kerosene cookers to heat water to blanch the almonds and to melt the chocolate! Oh, Peter, that's wonderful!"

Peter bought a secondhand cheese grater, a block of chocolate from the chocolate factory, almonds, and other ingredients with almost their last money. The window sill was just large enough to hold the kerosene stoves. They smelled terribly, especially when they were turned off, but it was an improvement over charcoal!

They went to the German club as soon as some of the confections were ready and got acquainted with several families. Their new acquaintances were eager to buy marzipan and chocolate candy. There they met Dr. Demerer, who gave them a book entitled *Receptarius Industriales* (Industrial Recipes); Mr. Wittmeier, a grandfatherly looking German, and Eddie, a young man who lived with him. Helen remembered Eddie from her growing-up years in Hamburg. He used to live close to her parents' house. It felt like a bit of home when the men came to visit.

They decided to stay with their marzipan and candy business. From the beginning their new venture was a huge success. A German baker ordered the marzipan by the kilo. Peter got so many orders at the German club that Helen kept busy the whole day.

Helen and Peter designed some white cardboard boxes with a blue stripe for one pound of candy. Peter bought some small brown paper cups, and some fancy colored aluminum foil, such as they use in Germany for packaging chocolate candy.

Helen invented her own recipes, some chocolate candy filled with marzipan or a mixture of marzipan, chocolate, and nuts, whole almonds, walnuts, dates, raisin heaps, and many others. She dipped them all by hand and packed them in the cartons. Peter sold them and looked for a job. After a while they bought a little camp stove which used gasoline, and she did not have to suffer any more from the noxious kerosene fumes.

One day Schneider arrived from Santo Domingo with the furniture. It was wonderful to sleep in a real bed and have chairs, a table to work on, and even a wardrobe to hang their clothes in!

The second Christmas away from home came. One day Peter came home with a two-foot-high paper Christmas tree and a little package.

"That's your Christmas gift," he smiled. Inside was a little soft, white, stuffed dog. "For the baby," he said.

That little stuffed dog was the best Christmas gift Helen ever had. Oh, how she looked forward to her very own little baby!

"Peter, what shall we name the baby? I hope it is a boy. I really would like a boy first. What do you think?"

They decided on the name *Dieter* (pronounced Deeter) for a boy. *Helga* was their choice for a girl.

The candy business dropped off a little after Christmas, but they had a regular income to cover their expenses. Then Peter came home one day, all smiles.

"I found a job today!"

"Oh, Peter, you did?! What kind of a job, and when do you start?"

"It's as a salesman for an agency that represents New York exporters. They also have stock of lady's dresses from a firm called Montgomery Ward. I can start the first of February."

"That's great! And just when the baby is due!"

"And the best is we can live in the servant quarters behind the office. I saw it. It's nothing fancy, but we don't have to pay any rent. I will not get a salary. It's only on a commission basis, but we'll do all right."

"Tell me how the rooms look. Is there a kitchen? And what else?"

"Well, there is a bedroom. It's small with only a screen over the window, no shutters or curtains or anything. There is a kitchen with a screened window and door and a real living-room. It even has a glass window. Can you imagine? And we can use the back patio with a nice roofed-over place where we can eat. The former occupants promised to vacate the rooms in time for us to move."

Schneider helped them move. They went on their way to the new location, again with a hand cart piled high with their furniture and their suitcases. But when they got to their new quarters, the people were still there, and they could not move in.

There they were, standing in the street with all their belongings on the hand cart. At last they were allowed to stash it all in the living-room. Someone told them of a little boardinghouse not far away, where they could stay until they were able to move in. The baby was due any day.

Chapter 8

Dieter

Peter and Helen had to stay in the boardinghouse until their promised quarters were vacated. But it took day after day, and they could not move in. In the morning of the sixth day Helen felt some strange sensations. She never had felt anything like that before.

"Peter, I think the baby wants to come," she said. "Please call the doctor and find out when I should go to the hospital."

Peter had a frown on his face when be came back. "I called the doctor, but I was told he is on his honeymoon, and when I asked if they could recommend another doctor who speaks English, they said they did not know any. How do you feel now?"

"I don't know. It feels funny, but I don't know how one is supposed to feel when a baby comes. Let's go to the hospital."

Peter took Helen's suitcase, and they walked the few short blocks to the hospital. She heard Peter arguing in Spanish with the attendants at the admittance office.

"Helen, there is no one who speaks English." He shook his head. "And they don't want me to come in with you. What shall we do? They told me to leave."

"Oh, Peter. I don't know. What can we do if they do not want you to come in with me? I have to be admitted. I think the baby is coming. I cannot stay out in the street."

Peter left. A nurse brought Helen to her room. A crib stood against the wall. She felt uneasy. How could she communicate with the doctor? She knew that her mother had a Cesarean section when she was born, and she did not have any idea what to do to deliver a baby.

The language barrier made the delivery very difficult, but at last the ordeal was over. Helen was alone in her room when she woke up from the anesthesia, and a baby lay in the crib at her side. But what was it, a boy or a girl? At last a nurse came into the room.

"Que is? (what is it)" Helen managed to say.

"Es un varon," came the answer.

She wondered, what was *un varon?* She knew that *un niño* was a boy, and *una niña* a girl, but never heard the word *varon* describe a baby. She thought *Varon* sounded like *Baron* in German. That would be a man. A woman would be *Baroness*. It must be a boy! A big flood of happiness engulfed her. Her own baby!

It was a good baby, seven and a quarter pounds. He fussed a little at first, but soon slept through the nights. But Helen could not get her strength back. At last the doctor told her that she had amoebas. She drank large quantities of tamarind tea, with a pleasant, fruity taste; and that took care of the problem. But she was still weak and could not take up the candy business again.

How fortunate that Peter got his job just in time. He was looking for customers the whole day.

Because the mosquitoes were not as numerous as in Haiti and Santo Domingo, Helen did not take any more quinine tablets. She was alone with the baby when she got a malaria attack. She had a horrible headache and chills. Her temperature went up to over 104°. There was no one to help and take care of her and the baby. She took Dieter in bed with her to take care of him as well as she could. The quinine tablets helped her to get over the attack, but she felt weak and tired again. It was no sense to try to make candy.

Letters from home came sparingly at that time and only through the Red Cross because of the war in Europe. In April a letter arrived with the news that Helen's mother had passed away in January. Helen grieved for her. She had not expected never to see her again when they left Germany! Her mother had not even known that they had a baby! Helen's heart felt heavy thinking about her. The only consolation was that her mother did not have to live through the awful war years in Hamburg.

Life seemed so meaningless. Why are we here? Why are we born? It did not make any sense. Dieter would grow up and die, just like she herself. What purpose was there in life? There was no Solution. Peter tried to reason with her, pointing out that there was a God, that there was purpose in life, but it made no sense to her. She could not believe.

Her comfort was her baby. Her heart overflowed with love for him. She cuddled his soft little body in her arms. Dieter was such a good baby. He seldom cried and had her mother's blue eyes. Helen felt a little better with the thought that she was now the mother.

She had plenty of time for reflections. Despite the happiness of having the baby she wished there were something more to fill that emptiness in her heart. She reread the books which she had brought from Germany. Among them was one about a Catholic family who had strong faith. She envied them, wishing that she could have faith like theirs. Her favorite book was *Christus Legenden,* by Selma Lagerloef, telling stories from Christ's childhood and other legends about Christ. It reminded her of the time when her girlfriend's mother had prayed with her, and she had believed in Jesus.

It had been in 1921 and Helen's second year in school, when she was seven years old. Food was scarce during the first world war and the years that followed. Helen was much too small and thin. She needed to gain some weight. Mrs. Schmidt, the mother of one of her girl friends, invited her to spend the summer vacation at their home in the country.

With her short, light-brown hair and grey eyes Helen felt like a little runt beside tall, blue-eyed Ellen with long blond curls. But she loved the country and the white, doll-sized house, shaded by a few tall trees. She liked the rhubarb plants growing in their shade, sheltering little green, wriggly frogs, and—on the sunny side—pansies in rainbow colors, and calendulas, the color of the setting sun. For her it was a special and wonderful time!

Mornings and evenings the air was filled with the songs of birds. Helen breathed in deeply the fresh air and smell of the pine trees.

The peaches were just ripe in time for them to eat! They felt heavy and velvety in her hand, and did they smell good! The juice dribbled down her chin.

What made the time extra special was that Mrs. Schmidt came to the girls' room in the evening, after they had gone to bed. She knelt at each of the girls' beds and prayed with them. She taught Helen a little prayer. In German it rhymed. In English it went something like this:

> I am small,
> My heart is clean,
> No one shall live in it
> But Jesus alone.

That was the first time anyone had prayed with her, and she liked it. She wanted to be good and please Jesus. When Helen came home she asked her mother to pray with her too, but after a few times it was forgotten.

But happiness filled her heart when she held Dieter. He was healthy, gaining weight, and starting to crawl around the secondhand playpen Peter had bought for him. His hair, black when he was born, gave way to little short blond hairs. And how his little face lighted up with a big smile when be got his first taste of orange juice!

Peter worked hard, but it was difficult to make a living. The agency represented some exporters from the United States, but the selection of offers Peter received was very limited, and he could not make enough sales. He bought a pretty yellow dress for Helen, but he could not sell many dresses or other items from Montgomery Ward's to other people. He had to find another way to support them.

Helen wrote letters by the hour to manufacturer's and export houses in different countries, trying to get their representation. At last offers came from a textile manufacturer in Nagasaki, Japan, a watch factory in Switzerland and some hardware wholesalers from New York. Peter quit his job at the agency and started his own business. He bought a little dark-blue Chevrolet from a secondhand dealer. How they enjoyed having a car again!

Peter had made the acquaintance of a German businessman who owned a house in town. Their new friend needed only the front room and a few rooms off the patio for his office and let Peter and Helen rent the rest: the roofed part of the patio, bedroom, bathroom, and kitchen.

They moved in the fall of 1940. Helen felt stronger and went back to candy making. For the first time in her marriage she had a real gas stove. How much easier it was than cooking on charcoal or with her little gasoline stove.

They had not seen their friends, Mr. Wittmeier and Eddie, for some time and were wondering about this. Then Mr. Wittmeier came to visit them a few days before Christmas. He came alone.

"How is Eddie?" Peter asked. "Why did he not come with you?"

Mr. Wittmeier looked at them with a shocked expression, "Oh, didn't you know? I thought you knew about it. Eddie died."

"No! Eddie died?" Helen stared at him. "What happened?! When did he die?!"

"Just a few weeks ago."

"But what happened? From what did he die?"

"Polio. A polio epidemic broke out several months ago. He got sick and died after a few days."

Tears welled up in Helen's eyes. She wiped them away with her hands.

Dieter was cranky a day before Christmas. He threw tantrums, something he had never done before. His forehead felt hot, and Helen brought him to the pediatrician living close by.

"Tonsillitis without complications," was his verdict. He gave her some nose drops for the baby and told her not to worry.

She gave Dieter the nose drops faithfully, but something was awfully wrong. In the evening the baby was listless, burning with fever.

"Look, Peter!" Dread clutched at Helen's heart. "Look at his leg. It seems that the color is different. It looks blue! What do you think?!"

They tried to call the doctor but could not reach him. A little later one of Dieter's arms took the same bluish color. Then the pupil of one eye dilated. But still the doctor could not be reached.

In the morning Helen called the doctor who had treated her for amoebas and malaria. He asked if Dieter had been born in his clinic, because he would only treat children born there. Even when she told him they didn't know him then, he refused to come.

Dieter got worse. His eyes rolled back in his head. Helen called the pediatrician again and told him the symptoms. At last he came and brought another doctor with him. One of the doctors started to examine him.

"Doctor, he is turning blue!" Helen screamed.

The doctor held Dieter in his arms. "Fill his bathtub with lukewarm water while I undress him."

After a while Dieter's color became normal again, but he was wrestling for breath.

"It's polio," one of the doctors said. Turning to Peter he added, "It is Sunday and not many pharmacies are open, but try to find one which is open and get some oxygen."

It took quite a time until Peter came back. The doctor fashioned a funnel from some newspaper to put over Dieter's face and connected the small oxygen tank to it, to help him breathe. In the meantime one of the doctors telephoned the children's hospital to have the baby admitted, but the hospital refused admittance. Then he telephoned the other hospitals in Caracas, but they, too, refused admittance. At last the isolation station out of town, at the side of the cemetery, consented to take the baby.

Helen cradled Dieter in her arms as Peter, with the horn screaming, raced behind the doctor's car. Dieter's breathing got more labored. At last they reached the hospital. They entered a little waiting room.

"Stay here." One of the doctors turned to them. "You cannot come in with us."

He took Dieter from Helen's arms. Both of the men disappeared into the hallway, closing the door behind them.

The small white waiting room smelled like antiseptic. The door through which the doctors disappeared had a window in the upper half. A few chairs stood close to the window. Some white coats hung on the wall. There was no counter or anything else, no one to admit the patients.

They waited for what seemed a long time, but no one came to tell them how Dieter was, or to have them fill out some forms for admittance. They looked through the window of the door, but there was no doctor, no nurse to be seen. At last Peter pointed to the coats.

"Helen, Let's put these on and see where Dieter is."

They entered the narrow hallway with doors on each side with large windows in them, so one could oversee the white-walled rooms. A little girl was sitting all alone on a low chair in one of the rooms. Otherwise, Helen did not see anyone. At last she saw through a window a bed against a wall and a little crib at the other wall. A baby was lying in the crib. They entered. It was their baby, all alone, fighting for breath.

Peter tried to help him breathe, admitting artificial respiration. Suddenly he grabbed him and put him over his shoulder. Helen looked in the baby's face. He did not labor for breath anymore. He was dead.

Peter held him close. After a while he put him on the bed. They were standing there, not knowing what to do. Then the doctor who had treated Helen came in.

"I have something here that sometimes helps." He fingered something in his breast pocket and shrugged, "But it's too late now."

He turned and left without another word. It took a long time before someone else appeared.

Helen felt numb. At last someone came in and informed them that the deceased had to be buried within twenty-four hours, and that women were not allowed at the cemetery during burial.

Peter called an acquaintance the next morning to help him bury the baby. Helen was alone at home. The few women with whom she had become acquainted were afraid to come. They had families and children of their own.

This was the end. There was no hope. She knew she would never see her little boy again, never again cradle his little body in her arms, never see his little grin again.

Her school in Germany had done too good a job of turning her into an atheist by teaching evolution. It never occurred to her there could be a God that she could pray to. For her there was no one to turn to. Her arms ached from being empty. She wanted to hold her baby. She was a mother and had no child. She cried when she saw children in the street.

She could not go to the cemetery; it hurt too much, and it was hard to be in the home where everything reminded her of Dieter. People told her that they were young and could have other children, but in her pain she did not want other children. She wanted Dieter, her own little baby who had died a week less then eleven months old.

The house was fumigated to sterilize it, and that was also the end of their candy business. They decided to move out of the city, to live somewhere where it would be healthier, where they could have a garden and be out in nature.

Chapter 9

Helga

Driving around with Peter and looking for a new place to locate was better than staying at home, where the pain over the loss of her baby overwhelmed Helen. But they looked for many weeks for a house to rent. There were very few houses available close to Caracas, and they either did not like them, or the price was beyond their means.

After they had spent another fruitless day searching for the right place, Peter said, "Helen, I think things will work out differently from what we expected. Maybe we should not rent, but try to have a house built for us."

"Build a house? We cannot afford that!"

"No, but I heard there are landowners in Chacao. It's a suburb about twenty minutes from town. They have large holdings and are dividing them, and the lots are not very expensive. We have to take a mortgage. Maybe we can pay the land off."

A few days later Peter drove their little blue Chevy to Chacao. They turned into a wide, dead-end street with a view of Mount Avila in the distance. Small, young trees, shrubs, and lush green lawns surrounded the modern light-colored, one-story houses with flat roofs. Some had chain link fences, others elaborate wrought iron fences with brick posts. They saw building sites scattered between them. Helen saw a woman in the front of the next house.

"I'm going to ask her who the owner of the building sites is," Peter said as he stopped the car and got out.

"You won't believe this," he said as he started the car again. "This is called San Marino. It's a part of Chacao. All these properties belong to an Italian who is also a builder. He builds the houses according to the buyer's specifications. The best is, he does the financing himself and charges only interest for the mortgage on the house. That is not more than paying rent! The woman told me where he lives. It's not far from here."

Peter drove the short distance to the house of the landowner. He was a tall, distinguished-looking gentleman. He drove them around the neighborhood, and they selected a piece of land in San Marino.

It was an exciting time making plans for the house. It was to be built of brick and stucco, like all the houses in Caracas, but with screens at the windows. Helen lay awake nights thinking of Dieter, thinking of the house. Maybe they should have another baby. No one ever could take the place of Dieter, but it would be easier if she could hold a baby again, and it would be so much healthier for the baby to be out in the country.

Helen drew the plans for the house. The two bedrooms, a den, and kitchen were to open into the living-room, with a maroon tile floor and off-white walls. No space would be wasted for a hallway.

"We need a veranda that we can sit outside," Helen said.

"And a high fence around the property," Peter added, "with a gate, so that we can have a dog. We can plant bougainvilleas, hibiscus, and the shrub with those broad reddish leaves like some of the hedges we saw."

In the meantime the infrequent letters from home continued to come through the Red Cross. One day Peter handed Helen a letter.

"Oh, Peter! It's from Ilse, my school friend in Hamburg! I have not heard from her for so long!" She tore open the envelope.

"Peter, listen what Ilse writes! She has a little boy, and he is so terribly undernourished. Because of the war they do not have sufficient to eat. She is afraid that he may die if she cannot get help. The doctor told her that he needs some special food, something called Biomalz, to strengthen him. I used to get that when I was little and undernourished, because of the shortage of food during the first world war.

"We got help from the Quakers from America. They sponsored school lunches for all us undernourished children. I remember the bean and potato soups; and, can you imagine, chocolate soup! We got a fat slice of delicious white bread with it every lunch. And my aunt sent packages to us from New York.

"Isn't there something like that now, so we can send food packages? I'm so glad, that we are here. Maybe we can help our friends and families now."

"Yes, there is," Peter nodded his head. "Just the other day I got an advertisement from a firm in New York who sends what they call Care Packages to Germany. We can order them. Maybe they can also send that Biomalz."

The months flew by quickly. Peter's agency business increased. He rented a small store close to the market, to be used as an office. Two large double doors folded against the inside, shelves lined the opposite wall. One long wooden counter reached almost from one side to the other, leaving just enough space for a couple of chairs and a small table for Peter's typewriter. He purchased hosiery, small leather goods, and other small items from local wholesalers, and employed a young girl to take care of the store. Peter was able soon to engage a salesman, Señor Garcia, for his wholesale business.

Then the baby was almost due. This time there was no language barrier for Helen. She met tall, white-haired Dr. Pepe Izquierdo through some acquaintances. Dr. Izquierdo had his own clinic, and by now Helen had picked up enough Spanish to enable her to communicate with him. The delivery would not be such a trauma.

"Helen, we cannot get a telephone for our new house," Peter said when the house was almost finished. "There are no more lines. What do we do now? "

"You have a telephone at your office, and I can ask our next-door neighbor if they will allow us to use their telephone in case of an emergency," she assured him. "I'd like to get acquainted with them anyway."

The neighbor lady graciously accepted Helen's request. The problem with the telephone was solved.

Moving day came. The living-room looked homey with a round mahogany table and dining room chairs made of bent aluminum tubes with rattan seats and backs. Peter bought the chairs from people returning to the United States. He also purchased a sofa and a very old, used piano. Later they found that it was riddled with termites. The furniture in Venezuela was build of solid mahogany, the native wood the termites would not attack. There was no danger the termites would attack the house. The only wood used in the building were the doors: the rest was build of brick and cement.

A lawn was planted in front of the house, and the hedge of bright red bougainvillea, hibiscus, and red-leaved shrubs. Peter planted tangerine trees all along the front, and in the back two avocados, a grapefruit, and a pomegranate tree, and some yellow roses in the middle of the lawn.

Helga was born in November, 1941, one day after Helen got her curtains up. She lay in the light, friendly room in Dr. Izquierdo's clinic, overflowing with joy. Her new baby lay asleep in her crib at the side of her bed. How wonderful to hold a baby again! She cuddled and loved her little girl who looked so much like the first baby, with a tiny mouth in its red little face, and the softest straight dark hair.

When she got home, Helen put the baby into the little white crib, all swathed in mosquito netting. She loved to care for Helga. But there was a fear in her heart. Would she ever be able to love with such abandon as she had loved her firstborn? Or would there always be the fear of suffering loss again? The pain had been too great; it was still there.

Peter bought a secondhand baby buggy, and Helen went on walks in the neighborhood, pushing the baby buggy. One day a slim, tall woman with two little blond girls came toward her. They started a conversation, and it turned out that she was also from Germany. Her name was Gertrud, and she lived only about two blocks away. Gertrud was married to an

Italian businessman. The little girls were six and three years old. Helen and Gertrud visited each other and went on walks together.

Germany declared war against the United States after the Japanese had bombed Pearl Harbor on December 7, 1941. Venezuela joined the Allies and declared war against Germany the next day, when Helga was a month old.

There had been no problems for Helen and Peter in Venezuela until then, but what would happen now? The uncertainty of their future worried Helen.

"Peter," she said at last, "I really would like to have a religion. You know that I brought some of my favorite books from Germany, and there is one about a Catholic family who really believes in God. What do you think about going to a Catholic priest, getting some instruction, and becoming a Catholic?"

"But, Helen, you know that I am a Lutheran."

"Yes, but God does not have much to do with our lives, and your father is a Catholic."

"Yes, but my mother is a Lutheran, and I was brought up as a Lutheran."

"But we never go to church, and I haven't met any Lutherans who live much differently than most other people. "

"Well, I don't know. There are Lutherans too who really believe."

"What if they put the German people into concentration camps as they did in Curacao during the first world war? Did they not put them on the island of Aruba? It must have been awfully hot there, and I don't want anything to happen to Helga."

Peter did not answer. He looked doubtful.

"Our neighbors are really nice. They are Catholics. I met them when I asked about the use of the telephone. I think that Mrs. Palacios may agree to be Helga's godmother if we become Catholics. They don't have any children of their own, and she likes Helga. What do you think?"

"I don't know," Peter said slowly.

"And if it comes to it that they intern the Germans, maybe I can bring Helga over to her. I know she would take good care of her. She seems to be so kind. I don't want anything to happen to our baby."

Peter shook his head. He did not say anything. He looked at the floor. At last he looked up and said, "Well, we can try."

"Let's find a priest who will instruct us," Helen said. "I don't want to wait. I really want to be able to believe."

Christmas came before they contacted a priest. Helga was a real comfort to Helen. How good to have her baby! Little blond curls took the place of the dark straight hair, and she was growing rapidly. It was fun to sew for her, and to go on walks with Gertrud and her two girls. In spite of her uneasiness about the future, Helen was happy. They had their income and she had her little one whom she loved so dearly, and she looked forward to becoming Catholics.

Chapter 10

God Intervenes

It was a few days after Christmas when Helen saw Peter getting slowly out of the car. His brows were creased. He did not greet her with his usual smile.

"What happened, Peter? You look worried. Is something wrong?" Helen put her hand on his shoulder and looked into his face.

"I can't believe it." Peter shook his head. "We are not involved in politics, and don't belong to any political party; and have not made any propaganda against the Allies. But I read in the paper today that we have been put on the proclaimed list."

"What does that mean, the *proclaimed list?*"

"It means, no one from the United States and Canada will deal with us as long as our name is on that black list."

"But why? Why did they put us on the list?"

"I don't know," Peter shook his bead. "But I'm going to find out, and I'm going to ask Dr. Simon, the lawyer, to help us to get off again. We haven't done anything wrong or harmed the Allies. I'm only glad we have the store. But Garcia, our salesman, told me that it would be better to have the store put in his name. Venezuela might consider confiscating all properties held by Germans. What do you think?"

"I don't know. I have never thought of that."

"I don't feel quite right about this." Peter shook his head. He looked troubled. "But what would we do, if the government really would confiscate all German properties?"

"Then they might also confiscate the house. Don't you think so, Peter?"

"That could be. But he didn't say anything about the homes. He especially mentioned the businesses."

"I really don't know. I don't know what will happen, and what would be the best to do. But he must know more about this country than we do. Maybe we should put the store in his name."

"I think so, too. I'll do it tomorrow." Peter said, but he still looked worried.

The worry proved to be justified. Peter came home early a few days later.

"Helen, please get ready to come with me to town. We are going to meet with Dr. Simon. You won't believe what that Garcia has done! I made a contract with him transferring the store to him, and this morning, when I came in the store, he told me to get out, that it was his store now! Can you imagine that! I think he is the one who told some lies about us to put us on the list so that he could get the store."

Helen took Helga, and went with Peter to the lawyer's office where Garcia and his lawyer were waiting. Garcia's lawyer presented the contract and asked if it was the contract Peter had set up. If it was, Peter did not have any more claim to the store.

"That's the contract," Peter said, "but I had it registered at the court house. It states Garcia did not pay anything for it, and that it is still my store."

Helen saw Garcia's mouth fall open. His lawyer looked at him and asked, "Is that true? You did not pay anything for the store? The contract is only a sham?" He looked at his client who avoided his eyes, and then said, "Man, you don't have a leg to stand on."

Garcia's lawyer stood up and shook his head while his client slunk out the door. Peter never saw Garcia again and continued working at the store.

Peter wrote to his firms that he was making efforts to get off the list. His firms in the United States and Canada promised to wait and not take another representative until he could work for them again. In the meantime, Peter had to make a living with the little store and hope that some of the Venezuelan merchants would deal with him.

"Helen," Peter said a few days later when he came home, "one of my customers, Mr. Gonzalez, invited us to a piñata, a birthday party for his little boy. I don't feel much like celebrating. What do you think?"

"We might as well go. It'll do us good to have a few hours without worry."

The afternoon of the birthday party arrived. Helen put on her yellow dress, dressed Helga in the little white dress she just finished, and combed her hair into a little curl on top of her head; then took her in her arms and got into the blue Chevy.

Peter drove to the city. He parked close to Mr. Gonzalez' house. Helen could hear the children laugh and shout as they entered the house through a short hallway.

People crowded the patio. Chairs lined the white painted stucco walls. Many children, big and small, gathered around a large rooster, fashioned of red, yellow, green, and orange crêpe paper, hanging from a rope strung from one side of the patio to the other.

The host, dark-haired, and with a smile in his dark eyes, welcomed them with outstretched hands. He was taller and heavier than most Venezuelans.

"Welcome to the piñata," his voice boomed. "Let me introduce you to some friends of mine. They are also from Germany."

He led them to a couple standing at the other side of the open patio. The man was very slender with receding hairline and friendly grey eyes behind metal-rimmed glasses. His pretty wife, in a dress matching her blue eyes, wore her long blond, curly hair turned up into a bun.

"Señor and señora Grünzeug," their host said, "these are señor and señora Eickmann. They are also from Germany."

After exchanging some courtesies, Peter went off with his new acquaintance. Helen pulled her wooden chair closer to his wife, holding Helga on her lap. Mrs. Grünzeug smiled at her.

"Do you have any children?" Helen asked.

"Yes, one boy, Willie. Over there." Mrs. Grünzeug pointed to a blond, blue-eyed boy, about eight years old.

They engaged in a lively conversation. How good to speak German with someone and not have to grope for words!

Mr. Gonzalez yelled, "Let's start the piñata!"

The children, beginning with the smaller ones, were blindfolded. They took turns, hitting the piñata with a long stick until the rooster broke, showering candy and small toys on the screaming children as they grabbed for the goodies. What a scramble!

The hostess served small corn-husk wrapped bundles, cake and red Jell-O when the time came for refreshments.

"What are these?" Helen pointed to the small bundles on her plate.

"They are tamales made of cornmeal. Open and taste them. They are good."

Helen peeled the corn-husk off. The little tamales tasted delicious with their spicy filling. She enjoyed her visit with Mrs. Grünzeug, talking about their children and their experiences in the new country. Time to go home came too early.

"I invited the Grünzeugs to come to our house next week," Peter said on the way home. "We had the most interesting conversation. He is Jewish and spent some time in a concentration camp in Germany before immigrating with his family to Venezuela. He was able to get out only because his wife is not Jewish and they already had their passports and entrance visa for Venezuela. He sells Christian books. He calls it 'canvassing.' He speaks to everyone he meets with enthusiasm about Jesus. I told him that you would be interested in hearing him too."

Helen looked forward to seeing their new friends again. She set the table on the veranda when the evening of the appointment came. She put Helga to bed and waited eagerly for their coming. At last the guests arrived.

"Welcome to our home." Helen shook Max's and Sophie's hands. "I'm so glad you could come." She turned to Max. "I want to hear what you talked about with my husband. He told me a lot about you."

They settled on the chairs around the little table and Helen served iced tea and cookies. The daylight dimmed. But it was still early enough before the heavy dew fell.

They talked about their experiences in Germany, and in their new country until they finished the refreshments. Helen enjoyed their conversation very much. She liked Max, and especially Sophie with her friendly smiles.

Then Max looked at Helen and said, "Your husband told me that you don't believe in God. Is that true?"

"Yes, it is. I believe in evolution. I don't believe in God. I wish I could."

"Helen, you look around you and see that there is order in things. Everything in the world and in the universe is controlled by certain laws. Can you imagine what chaos would result if the stars would not be controlled by laws? Who do you suppose made those laws?"

Helen looked up at the sky. The moon had not appeared, and the stars shone brightly.

"Oh, those are laws of nature."

"Yes, that is right. But these laws of nature have to be made by someone. Laws don't come by themselves. There must be a lawmaker if there are laws. Don't you think so?"

"I guess so." She shook her head. "I never thought about that."

"We call the intelligence, the One who made the laws of nature, 'God.' "

She didn't answer. She thought about that. That was something that had never occurred to her. It made sense. Where there are laws there ought to be a lawmaker. Why not call that intelligence God instead of nature?

At last Helen looked up. "I suppose that would be all right."

"If you don't believe in creation," Max continued, "then tell me, where does the earth come from?"

That was easy, she thought. "From the sun."

"Where does the sun come from?"

"From the dust in the universe."

"Where does the dust in the universe come from?"

She looked down. She felt perplexed. She had never thought of that. It was like facing a dead-end. Where did the dust in the universe come from? Where did everything come from? Could it be that her teachers in school had taught error with their theory of evolution? The teachers were not stupid. She admired them. They had studied sciences. Could they have been so wrong? But where did anything come from? There was no answer in evolution!

At last Helen looked up again, and shook her head. "I don't know."

Max was not through with his questioning. "And when you don't believe in creation, just tell me, What was first, the egg or the hen?"

Helen felt bewildered. What was first? The egg or the hen? The hen had to come out of an egg, but a hen had to lay the egg! The egg could not come by itself! She could not figure it out. Where did the hen come from if it didn't come from an egg? It was not possible for a hen to evolve without an egg. Could it really be that there was a God who created everything?

She looked up at the sky again. The stars seemed brighter and closer than ever. Who made them? Who made the laws governing them? She did not understand. Could it be that there really was a God who created everything? Would it not be wonderful if there really was a God? How she wished she could believe!

A strange feeling of peace came over her. Helen looked up again at the sky ablaze with stars. Suddenly she felt like something touching her right shoulder.

"I believe!" she said.

Happiness filled her heart. It seemed that someone had taken hold of her hand. The emptiness she felt so long was gone. Yes, there was a God! It was true that there was a God! It was not all uncaring emptiness. Her heart felt like bursting with happiness.

Max interrupted her thoughts. "Would you like to know more about God?"

"Yes, oh, yes!"

"Would you like to study the Bible?"

Helen looked at Peter and with gladness heard his answer, "Yes, we would. I do have a Bible. I must find it. It must be somewhere."

"Then it's agreed," Max said. "When do you want to start?"

"As soon as we can." Peter seemed to share her eager feelings.

"Well, how about the day after tomorrow? We can come at the same time in the evening."

"That sounds great," Peter said. "We're looking forward to it."

Their friends left. Helen smiled, thinking of God! What a difference it made! She did not have to be afraid of the future, and studying the Bible would help her to know more about God.

Chapter 11

Letters from God?

Helen waited anxiously for Max and Sophie to come again. She had so many questions for which she did not have an answer.

Max, trim and neat in his white suit and dark necktie, Sophie in a white skirt and blue blouse, arrived two days later. He carried a small projector and a little black case.

"I'm so glad you came," Helen said, serving ice tea and cookies again. "I want to know more about the Bible. I'm so happy to be able to believe in God! But there is so much I want to know!"

"I have a question for you," Max said after a while. "If you have a friend, and he sends you his letters, would you read them?"

"Of course we would read them!" Peter replied.

"You know, Peter and Helen, God sent his letters to his people. It tells us in Timothy 3:16: That the scriptures are given by inspiration of God. The Bible is His letters to us."

"Then we had better read the Bible to find out what God wants us to do," Helen said.

"Yes, it is a pity how little we read God's letters. Now tonight I would like to show you some slides of the prophecies from the Bible. They are easier to understand when you can see them."

They went into the house to set up the projector. The house felt warm and cozy from the sun shining on its bricks all day.

"Let's sit here," Helen motioned to the rattan chairs around the table. They turned the chairs to face the screen.

"In order really to understand the Bible we ought to go back to the Old Testament," Max said. "Jesus admonished us to study the Scriptures, and at that time there was only the Old Testament. If the former prophecies are fulfilled, we can assume that the ones for the future will be fulfilled also. Don't you think so?"

"That sounds reasonable," Peter agreed.

"It is best to start our studies with the book of Daniel 2, in the Old Testament. Here, thousands of years ago, God told us about the end of the world. It is about a dream of King Nebuchadnezzar, king of Babylon. Do you remember Babylon's hanging gardens were one of the seven wonders of the world?"

"Yes," Helen said, "I remember we learned that in school."

Looking for a Better Country

Max turned the projector on. A tall, strange image of a man appeared on the screen. Helen listened fascinated as Max read that the image was made of different kinds of metals, starting with a head of gold, representing Babylon.

Medo-Persia, Greece, and then Rome were represented by a succession of inferior types of metal. Until the feet were a mixture of iron and clay.

"Remember," Max asked, "that Kaiser Wilhelm, the Czar of Russia, Queen Victoria of England, and all the other royal houses are related to one another? And here, in this book written so many years ago, it says they would mingle themselves with the seed of men but they will not succeed in establishing another world power, just like iron and clay don't stick together.

"Various powerful leaders, like Charlemagne and Napoleon, tried it, but they were not successful. Hitler will also not succeed. There never will be a united Europe again, not for any length of time, in spite of wars and treaties."

Helen listened spellbound as Max continued to read that a stone was cut out without hands, hitting the image upon his feet and broke it to pieces. The image became like chaff and the wind carried it away. The stone became a great mountain and filled the whole earth. At that time God would start setting up his kingdom. Then the end of the world would come and Jesus would return to take His people to heaven. The wicked would be destroyed.

"There will be no more suffering and death in the future life in heaven or later on the earth made new." Max said. "We are living now at the time of the feet mixed with clay."

"But then the end is really very close!" Helen said in surprise. "I didn't know that there is so little time left! I thought it would take millions of years."

"Yes, that's what many people think. But the Bible says differently. The end will come soon."

Helen shook her head and asked, "But when? What will happen?"

"It says in Matthew 24:14," Max replied, "that the gospel of the kingdom shall be preached in all the world for a witness unto all nations and then will the end come.

"But we don't have to be afraid. Listen to the Lord's promise in John 14:1-3:

" 'Let not your hearts be troubled: ye believe in God, believe also in me. In my Father's house are many mansions: if it were not so, I would have told you. I go to prepare a place for you. And if I go and prepare a place for you, I will come again and receive you unto myself; that where I am, there ye may be also.'

"You see, the Lord will save us, and there will be no more suffering or death in the future life in heaven or on the earth made new. We only have to be faithful. It says in the last book of the Bible, in Revelation 14:12:

" 'Here is the patience of the saints: here are they that keep the commandments of God and the faith of Jesus.' "

With that Max stood up, and put the projector away, and said, "Next time we will study more about these kingdoms."

Before they left Max and Sophie promised to come twice a week to study with them. In the meantime Helen took Peter's Bible and started to read it through as fast as she could. She and Peter could not learn fast enough, and drank in the studies like dry sponges.

The next time Max showed them that God had told Daniel the names of the kingdoms which were to come. "Greece is mentioned in Daniel 8:21 long before it became a world power. Before that another prophet had written about King Cyrus more than a hundred years before he was born."

"Then God knows the future!" Helen said in surprise.

"Yes," said Max. "God is omniscient. He knows the end from the beginning. There are many important things people don't know. Therefore we have to study, to find out what God wants us to know."

Awe struck Helen when she thought about how God had led them out of Germany. He had looked out for them. He had provided for their needs. He had led them to the department store in Belgium where Peter bought the folding chairs and the soft leather suitcases for them to sleep on, when they came to Venezuela. How would they have been able to make the chocolate candy without the cookbook and the beautiful scale?

In so many instances God had guided them! Her heart was filled with love for a God who had cared for them so much, even when they were not serving Him.

Every study brought new wonders. Helen no longer worried about their future. She was happy. She had her little baby. The store at the market brought enough income to cover their expenses.

One day Peter and Helen met other Christians and studied with them too. Hope sprang up in Helen's heart when she thought of her little boy.

"I'm so glad that we became Christians." She said when Max and Sophie came the next time, "Now I know that Dieter is in heaven and we will see him again."

"Well," answered Max, "you will see your baby again if you are faithful, but let's study what the Bible says about death.

"The Bible calls death *a sleep.* We read in 1 Thessalonians 4:13, and 16 and 17 that the Lord will descend from heaven with a shout of the archangel, and with the trump of God. The dead in Christ will rise and we will be caught up in the clouds together with them to meet the Lord in the air, and we will forever be with the Lord."

"You mean we don't go to heaven when we die?"

" That's right, Helen. God's faithful people who have died will be resurrected, and the living translated. Then the Lord will take us to heaven together, as it says here. You see, Helen, you will have your baby back. It will be resurrected when the Lord comes to take the redeemed home."

"But the Bible says," Peter frowned, "the soul goes to heaven when one dies, doesn't it?"

"You are right. Something is going back to God at death, Peter. To find out what it is, please read to us Ecclesiastes 12:7."

Peter read:

"Then shall the dust return to the earth as it was, and the spirit shall return unto God who gave it."

"See, Max," Peter looked at him, "it says the spirit goes back to God!"

Helen listened anxiously to the discussion. She had been happy with the thought that Dieter was now in heaven. But was it true?

"Remember how man was created in the beginning?" Max asked. "We read in Genesis 2:7 that the Lord formed him of the dust of the ground, and breathed into his nostrils the breath of life? It says that he *became a living soul,* not that God gave him a soul.

"A person is a combination of the dust of the ground and God's breath of life. The Hebrew word for soul here is *Ruach.* It is the same word which is used to describe the breath of animals in Ecclesiastes 3:19. It says there that men and animal have all one breath; so that a man has no preeminence above a beast.

"I'll give you an example, so you can understand better what happens when a person dies. If you want to make a box, you use some pieces of wood and some nails. There is no box before you start your work. Then you put the nails into the pieces of wood and fashion a box. The box is going to be there as long as wood and nails are together. Suppose you take the nails out. Where is the box? It is gone. So it is when the breath of life goes back to God: a dead body stays behind.

"See, Christ's tomb was empty after He was risen. Enoch and Elijah were taken to heaven. They did not leave any dead bodies behind. But what about all the other people? Their graves are not empty. Our bodies, too, will be changed when Jesus comes back. We will be translated and go with him. The graves of his faithful will be empty. But until then we will be sleeping in our graves."

"That makes sense," Helen said. "But there is one thing I don't understand. How could Jesus tell the thief on the cross he would be with

Him in paradise the same day he died, when he was supposed to be asleep until the resurrection?"

Max did not seem perturbed. "In our Bible it says, 'verily I say unto thee, today shalt thou be with me in paradise.'

"Do you know, Helen, in the original language there were no commas? The punctuation was added later and was not inspired. At that time the people believed they would go to heaven when they died, therefore they put the comma there. But see what happens when we shift the comma. Then that sentence reads: Verily I say unto thee today, thou shalt be with me in paradise.

"Then our baby is still asleep! That is not so bad. At least he is not suffering anymore, and we will be together when Jesus comes. I want to be faithful so I can have my baby again!"

"It is a blessing for our loved ones to sleep until the Lord comes," Max added. "Can you imagine if a husband who dies could look down on the earth and see his widow and children mourn and having a hard time? Maybe the children will get into trouble. Heaven would not be a happy place for him. Is it not far better just to sleep and get reunited with our loved ones when the Lord comes?"

Helen shook her head, "There are so many things I didn't know. I wonder what else there is to learn."

Chapter 12

From Store to Chicken Farm

Helen nursed her baby for about four months. Then she contracted a bad cold.

"Peter," she said, "I'm afraid to nurse the baby. I'm afraid she might catch my cold. I think it's better to get some milk from our new neighbors. They have a dairy. I'm sure we can buy some milk from them."

But Helga did not do well on the cow's milk. Besides, she ran a high fever a few days later.

"She has inflammation of the urethra," the doctor diagnosed her. "Also, the milk she is getting seems to be watered down. It's better to give her baby formula."

The little girl did well on the new formula, but Helen felt bad she was not nursing her longer. She determined to nurse a future baby as long as she could, so it would not get sick.

Helen was alone most of the time, because Peter left early in the morning and came back late at night. She looked forward to the evenings when Max and Sophie came. One study was about the creation of the Earth, from Genesis, the first book of the Bible.

"Jesus was with God the Father, at the creation of the Earth," Max said. "The word for God in the original language is *Elohim,* plural. He said in Verse 26, 'Let US make man in OUR image....' Later on, at the beginning of the gospel of John, we read: 'and the Word became flesh and dwelt among man....' "

"I know that Jesus died for us," Helen said, "but I did not know that He was also the creator of heaven and earth!"

"Yes, He is, and to think that He—the Creator—loves us so much that He suffered and died for us on the cross. He died for our sins."

"What does it really mean, to sin?" Peter asked.

"You can read what the definition for sin is in the first letter of John 3:4. 'Whosoever committeth sin transgresseth also the law: for sin is the transgression of the law.' "

"That means the new laws which Jesus gave us, doesn't it? It does not mean the old Ten Commandments. We heard that the laws of the Old Testament were nailed to the cross."

Max nodded his head in agreement. "I know that it says in the New Testament that the handwriting of ordinances was nailed to the cross. It is a favorite text some use to try to show that the Ten Commandments are

56

not in force any more; but in Deuteronomy 10, in verses 1-2, the Lord told Moses to hew two tables of stone like the first, and He would write on them the words written on the first, which Moses had broken, and he should put those tables of stone into the ark.

"In Deuteronomy 31:24-26 it tells us how Moses, when he had made an end of writing in a book all that the Lord had told him, commanded the Levites, who carried the ark of the covenant to take the book of the law, and put it in the side of the ark....

"You see, Peter, there is a difference between the ordinances, written by Moses, and the Ten Commandments, written by God himself."

"But," Helen interrupted, "what about the new commandment? I heard that Jesus said He would give us a new commandment. I wrote the text down. It is in Matthew 22:37–40, and it says: 'Thou shalt love the Lord thy God with all thy heart, and with all thy soul, and with all thy mind. This is the first and great commandment. And the second is like unto it, thou shalt love thy neighbor as thyself.' "

"Helen, do you know, these commandments are not new?" Max asked. "Please read to us Deuteronomy 6:5."

Helen opened her Bible and read, " 'And thou shalt love the Lord thy God with all thine heart, and with all thy soul, and with all thy might.' I didn't know that this was already in the Old Testament!"

"Now turn to Leviticus 19:18. What does it say there?"

"Thou shalt love thy neighbor as thyself." She shook her head and looked at Max. "These commandments are not new!"

She shook her head again. "I didn't know that. There are so many things I didn't know about the Bible, and we had Bible in school; but we never heard anything like this."

Max continued. "Matthew 5:18 says that 'till heaven and earth pass, one jot or one tittle shall in no wise pass from the law, till all be fulfilled.' Heaven and earth are still here, aren't they?"

"Do you really think that the old Ten Commandments are still in force?" Peter asked.

"It is not what I think, but what the Bible says that is important," Max continued. "There is another text I would like you to read. It is in the very last book of the Bible, in Revelation 14:12: 'Here is the patience of the saints: here are they that keep the commandments of God, and the faith of Jesus.'"

"It says, 'the commandments of God,' " Peter stroked his chin. "And in the very last chapter of the Bible. You mean then that we still have to keep the old Ten Commandments? But doesn't it say in the Bible that Jesus fulfilled the law?"

Max said, "Jesus fulfilled the law, but that does not mean that He did away with it. He obeyed it. Besides, which laws would not be in force now? Should you still honor your father and mother? Is it right to kill, steal, commit adultery, covet your neighbor's belongings? No. The same goes for the laws pertaining to God. Are you to take his name in vain, have other Gods before him, pray to idols, or desecrate the holy day? Of course not."

"That sounds as if they are still in force," Peter admitted.

" That's right," Max opened his Bible and said, "Let's read the Ten Commandments. They are in Exodus 20:3–17."

They started to read. Peter shook his head: "But they are different from the ones I learned in school from the Catechism of the Lutheran church."

"That's right," Max said. "Men have made some changes in them. The second commandment, about not making any graven images and praying to them, was taken out. The tenth commandment was cut in two in order to still have ten. The fourth commandment became the third. In the Catechism it says only: 'Keep holy the holiday,' but look what it says in the Bible in verses 8 to 11:

" 'Remember the sabbath day, to keep it holy. Six days shalt thou labor, and do all thy work: but the seventh day is the sabbath of the Lord thy God: in it thou shalt not do any work, thou, nor thy son, nor thy daughter, thy manservant, nor thy maidservant, nor thy cattle, nor thy stranger that is within thy gates: for in six days the Lord made heaven and earth, the sea, and all that in them is, and rested the seventh day: wherefore the Lord blessed the sabbath day, and hallowed it.' "

Peter looked stunned. "But isn't Sunday the day to keep holy? Isn't it the seventh day?" he asked. "The week starts with Monday."

"That's how we learned it in Germany." Max agreed, "But what does the Bible say? We ought to go by what the Bible says.

"In German it is clear, which day is the seventh. The fourth day is called *Mittwoch. Mitte* is middle. The word *Woche* is week. Mittwoch can be only the middle of the week when the first day is Sunday, and Saturday is the seventh day.

"In Spanish it is clear too, which day is the seventh, the Sabbath. The word for Saturday is *Sabado.*

"But I heard that a day of creation was 1,000 years," Helen said. "Why is it so important to keep the literal day, when a 1,000 years was one day?"

"I know that some people teach that about creation," Max explained, "but I don't think that their version has much merit. We read that evening and morning was one day at creation. Evening, or the dark part of the day, would be 500 years if a day was 1,000 years. God created the trees, and plants on the third day, the fish and fowl on the fifth, and the other animals on the sixth day. It is not very likely that they would have survived 500 years of darkness.

"God rested the seventh day after He created man. He declared the seventh day holy and forbade all work on it. Adam died when he was 930 years, but God had told him in Genesis 3:23 'to till the ground from whence he was taken.' That does not make any sense if Adam was to keep the Sabbath holy for 1,000 years."

Peter looked down at the floor. He held his chin in his hand. When he looked up he asked, "Is it really so important to keep the Sabbath on Saturday? Can't one keep it on Sunday like other Christian denominations?"

"Peter, let me give you an example," Max said. "Suppose there are seven glasses, all equal in size and shape. The seventh has water in it. The others are empty. You are thirsty and reach out to drink. Does it matter which glass you take? If you take any of the first six, your thirst will not be quenched. Only when you take the seventh will you be satisfied. God hallowed only the seventh day. Do you believe that it makes any difference which day you will keep?"

"So, you really mean that Saturday is the Sabbath day of the Bible?"

"Yes, I do," Max affirmed.

Helen looked at Peter. There was turmoil in her heart. What were they supposed to do? She knew Saturday was the day people did their buying. Their income came now only from the little store at the market. She knew no store was allowed to open on Sundays. What would Peter do?

Peter looked down again. He shook his head. He did not say anything. At last he looked up. "It looks like we still have to keep the fourth commandment," he said slowly. "We want to obey God. But then we probably cannot keep our store after all. Saturday is the day people come to buy. They get paid on Fridays. There is a law here in Venezuela that forbids having a store open on Sunday, and by Monday nobody has any money left."

Helen looked at her husband. "But, Peter, how shall we live?"

"I don't know. I don't know." He shook his head. "I don't know what will happen, but one thing is sure: if God says that we have to keep the Sabbath holy, we have to close the store on Sabbath."

They sat silently. At last Max interrupted Helen's thoughts with: "How about starting a chicken farm?"

"A chicken farm?!" Helen stared at him. "We don't know anything about chickens! I have never even touched a live chicken!"

She heard Peter say, "Max, we grew up in Hamburg, Germany. Hamburg is a large city. People don't have chickens in Hamburg. We don't know the first thing about them."

"We can show you," came the cheerful reply. "We have some chickens. The Lord will bless and help you if you obey Him. It is not difficult. You have quite a large piece of land behind your house. You can build some chicken houses, and you can probably get the chickens from the place we got ours. They are good chickens. You can get an incubator and raise more chickens, later selling the eggs and the young roosters. But let's pray that God will lead you in your decision."

Peter's eyes looked troubled. "Helen," he said after Max and Sophie left. "What do you think? What about a chicken farm? Do you think that we can handle it?"

"Peter," she sighed and shrugged her shoulders, "I don't know. The only thing is to pray about it some more. See how it turns out when you close the store on Sabbath."

It turned out that Peter was right. The store brought only enough to pay the rent and the telephone. There was no way they could earn enough to make a living with it. They decided to sell it.

Helen thought about the candy business, but their expenses were so much greater now than when they first arrived in Caracas. They had the interest to pay for the mortgage, the baby, and another on the way. Helen doubted that they could build up the candy business fast enough to meet expenses.

"I found a buyer for the store," Peter said a few days later when he came home "We don't get much out of it. He does not have much money. I'm taking some of the wallets and sewing kits out, and other small things. Maybe we can sell them later. We are only keeping our post office box. I don't see another way than to try the chicken farm."

A friend of Max helped them to build a chicken house and a fenced-in place in the yard. Max went with Peter to buy twelve Rhode Island Red hens and a rooster.

That rooster was something to behold! It was the largest, most beautiful and colorful rooster Helen had ever seen. His long tail feathers shone like a rainbow in the sunshine. His crowing woke them up early in the morning.

Peter bought an incubator. Helen filled it with freshly laid eggs, and turned each egg faithfully every day. At last the day came when the chickens hatched. They watched fascinated as the little chicks emerged from their shells. They looked a little wet and bedraggled, but soon little fluffy chickens peeped to their hearts' content. Helen held them in her hand. How light they were, so soft and wriggly and full of life! She put them into their brooder, and they grew rapidly.

"Helen," Peter said a few weeks later, "I heard that White Leghorns lay more eggs than the Rhode Island Reds. One can order eggs, ready to hatch, from New York. I'm going to order some of the Leghorn eggs."

The shipment arrived a few days later. The eggs came in large flat boxes, with many holes on the sides. Peter opened the boxes carefully.

"Look, Peter," Helen cried, "there are tiny cracks appearing in the shells. They are hatching already!"

The chicken farm never got very large, but at least they had some income from it. They cleaned and prepared the young roosters, and wrapped them in cellophane paper, for the market, when they were large enough to tell them apart from the hens. They kept the hens to increase their egg production.

Max and Sophie came one Sabbath afternoon, and Helen said, "I'm so tired today. I worked last night until ten o'clock in order to be able to keep the Sabbath."

Max showed them from the Bible that the Sabbath is from sundown to sundown, not midnight to midnight. Helen never worked until 10 p.m. on Friday again.

Chapter 13

God Keeps His Word

The studies continued. They were the highlights of Helen's days. One evening Max said, "I want to invite you to come to church next Sabbath. We are going to have a guest speaker from America. He and his wife speak English. You'll like them."

"Go to church?" Peter raised his eyebrows. "I never thought of that."

"Well, we have studied now for several months, and it would strengthen your faith to associate with others who believe as you do."

"I guess, you are right." Peter smiled. "What do you think, Helen?"

"Maybe we should go and see if we like it."

"Where is the church?" Peter turned to Max. "And when does it start?"

"It's in the middle of town. I'll write the address down for you. It starts at eleven o'clock. We'll be waiting at the door."

Helen did not have much trouble making a selection of what to wear. The top of her yellow dress had worn out. She cut it off and sewed an off-white top for it. She liked it even better than when it was all yellow. She dressed Helga in her little white dress, and combed the baby's blond curls into a little curl on top of her head.

Peter drove the little blue Chevy to town. They turned into the street where the church was located. It was crowded between two other buildings in a residential part of Caracas. Iron bars protected the windows. Over the wide-open double door was a large sign: "Iglesia Adventista del Septimo Dia" (Seventh-day Adventist Church).

Max and Sophie welcomed them with outstretched hands. A row of benches occupied the one side of the sunny patio.

"The members eat their lunch here while they wait for the afternoon meeting, and weekdays it is used by the dentist," Max said, pointing at a door behind the benches. "That door leads to a dental clinic sponsored by the church."

Max led them into the hall, filled with light-colored wooden pews on both sides, crowded with people. Most of the men wore meticulously clean white linen suits and ties, the women apparently their best dresses. The light-painted walls made a pleasant contrast to the dark-red drapes behind the pulpit. About a dozen people occupied some benches behind a piano.

One young man offered Peter and Helen his seat. An older lady proffered them her song book. The crowd sang enthusiastically. Helen held Helga in her arms. The baby seemed fascinated by what was going on and never cried. After the singing the tall, middle-aged speaker, dressed in a dark-blue suit, went to the podium to speak. Helen listened spellbound! She enjoyed the sermon and the singing.

After the meeting Max introduced them to the speaker. He stretched out both hands to Peter.

"God is looking for you, young man," he said as he shook Peter's hand.

Then Max introduced them to the white-haired, fatherly-looking pastor and his wife. Pastor Sherman shook Helen's hand, his eyes smiling at her behind his glasses. Mrs. Sherman, short, in a neat dark dress, wore her gray hair in a knot. Her friendly greeting made Helen feel at home. She liked the pastor and Mrs. Sherman. They met several members.

"These are the Vitos." Max introduced them to another couple. He was short and stocky with brown, curly hair, dressed in a light colored suit. She, a little taller and slender, wore a flowered dress.

"Brother Vito is the secretary of the mission. He is from Spain and his wife from Switzerland. You can speak German with her. They are here with their three children. The children attend the church school in the back of the church."

It was easy to become friends with the Vitos. They lived in town, and Sister Vito baked the most delicious bread to add to their income. Helen liked the friendly people of the church. It was comforting to have friends when times were difficult. It made a special impression on her to hear the members call each other "hermano" (brother) and "hermana" (sister).

They continued their study twice a week until William Baxter, a young American evangelist from Monte Morelos, Mexico, came to town. He held meetings five evenings a week. Peter agreed to take care of Helga, and Helen was able to attend the meetings of Pastor Baxter. On Sabbath they went to church.

Pastor Baxter with his wife Betty, and their little daughter Dadsy, visited Peter and Helen, and befriended them. Their help with the studies made it easier to make some difficult decisions.

"I didn't know that one has to pay tithe," Peter said, when the matter of tithing came up. " Isn't that only for the Jews, and during the time of the Old Testament?"

"Well, let's read what Jesus said about it, " answered Max. "Helen, do you want to read Matthew 23:23?"

"Woe unto you, scribes and Pharisees, hypocrites! For ye pay tithe of mint and anise and cumin, and have omitted the weightier matters of the law, judgment, mercy and faith: these ought ye to have done, and not leave the other undone."

"You see," Max looked at Peter, "Jesus said that it was right to pay tithe, a tenth of what you earn, even on the smallest things; but that law, judgment, mercy, and faith were even more important.

They read some more texts regarding tithes. Max showed them the text in Malachi 3:8–11:

" 'Will a man rob God? Yet ye have robbed me. But ye say, Wherein have we robbed thee? In tithes and offerings. Ye are cursed with a curse: for ye have robbed me, even this whole nation. Bring ye all the tithes into the storehouse, that there may be meat in mine house, and prove me now herewith, saith the Lord of hosts, if I will not open you the windows of heaven, and pour you out a blessing, that there shall not be room enough to receive it. And I will rebuke the devourer for your sakes, and he shall not destroy the fruits of your ground; neither shall your vine cast her fruit before the time in the field, saith the Lord of hosts.' "

"With the Lord's blessings, " Max said, "the nine-tenths of your earnings will go farther than if you would not return your tithe. See, it says here, it belongs to God. You are only returning to Him what is His, and you will have a blessing when you do it. The Lord is going to keep His word. Consider what Jesus gave for you! He came from heaven to live among men, and gave His life! The tithe is not much in comparison."

Helen wondered what Peter would do. Their earnings were not much. Most of the weeks it came to about 30,00 Bolivar (less than $10,00), but they agreed to return the tithes for the support of the ministry.

A few evenings later Max asked, "Would you like to join and become members of the church?"

Peter looked at Helen. She nodded her head in agreement, and in June, 1942, Peter and Helen took their stand and were baptized in the baptistry of the church.

Peter paid his tithes faithfully, but it was difficult making a living. Helen was glad that they had some income from the chicken business. On Sundays Helen went with Betty Baxter to sell the Spanish edition of the *Sings of the Times,* called El *Centinela,* a Spanish paper, dealing with many interesting topics of health and other subjects.

"The chicken business does not bring in enough to support us, Helen. " Peter shook his head. "I heard that one can sell some food at the factories at noon. I think we should sell the car and buy a little panel truck. I can put a small showcase in the back and get some things at the bakery to sell."

Peter bought an almost new-looking little dark-blue panel truck. Every noon he went to sell his wares at the factories, and Sundays at the ball games. It helped to augment their income. But when August came, all the chickens molted, and Helen had to buy eggs even for their own use.

Fortunately food was inexpensive. Two "fruteros" passed along their street with their horse-drawn open carriages. They sold for one "medio" (a quarter of a Bolivar) "verdura," consisting of a piece of cabbage, winter squash, some sweet potato, and other root vegetables, ocumo, ñame, mapoy, and pieces of yucca. It made a good vegetable stew with some home-grown carrots, onions and tomatoes. She cooked rice instead of potatoes, which was much cheaper, and increased in volume when it was cooked! She prepared tasty black beans, and plantain. They had plenty of eggs, most of the time.

One day Peter handed Helen a colorful catalog with pictures of luscious fruits and vegetables on the cover.

"I got this seed catalog from New York in the mail today, " he announced. "We can look through it and make an order ready after supper."

Helen did the dishes and put little Helga into her crib. Then they pulled their chairs up to the table to look at the catalog. The pictures of the trees and shrubs were beautiful, and the ones of the fruits and vegetables made Helen's mouth water.

"There are so many, Peter. I don't know what we should order."

"Look at this, " came Peter's reply. "It is called broccoli. We didn't have that in Germany."

"It looks good, " Helen responded. "Let's order that. And look at this okra. That's something new too. Let's order it with our carrots, radishes, and the other seeds."

"It will save on expenses, when we can grow all our own vegetables." Peter said, "The soil is so fertile. I'll bet they will grow in no time."

It was fun to prepare the beds for the new arrivals, then see the little sprouts come up! The broccoli had leaves in a few short weeks. Helen used the leaves of the broccoli as soon as they got a little larger. They were kind of tough, but tasted pretty good.

They planted okra. After harvesting the pods, Helen cooked it in salt water, and served it at dinner.

"Do you like this?" Peter asked. "These things are slimy. I sure don't like them."

"No, I don't like them either. " She shook her head. That was the end of the okra for them.

They bought bread from Sister Vito. It was heavier and more filling, and quite an improvement over the light, white French bread commonly used in Caracas. They put radishes and mustard greens on it instead of luncheon meats.

"The chicken feed is too expensive," Peter said one day. "I wonder if we cannot make our own chicken feed. Remember the *Receptario Indus-*

triales (Industrial Recipes), which Dr. Demerer gave us when we came here? Maybe there is a recipe in it for chicken feed."

What a blessing the book became to them! Peter studied it and found the recipe. He bought an electrical grinder and all the necessary ingredients to make his own chicken feed. After a while Peter was able to sell chicken feed to others. At times, that was their only income, besides Peter's sales of cakes, especially when the chickens molted and did not lay any eggs for almost a whole month.

The day came when Peter needed an ingredient for the chicken feed which came from Maracay, a town in the interior of Venezuela. He went to a transport company and gave his order. They told him to go to the garage from where the trucks left for Maracay and speak with the driver himself because he was supposed to leave shortly. But the day the order was to be delivered, Peter came home empty-handed.

"Helen," Peter looked serious and shook his head, "I don't know what to do. The man in the office had said that I should go over to the garage and give the check to the driver of the truck which went to Maracay, because he was to leave shortly. When I went today to the office to ask for the shipment, he told me that they could not deal with us because we were on the black list. He refused to give me back the check.

"What do we do now? We cannot finish the chicken feed, and we don't have enough money to order somewhere else! What shall we do?"

"We can pray about it," Helen answered. "And let's ask Max and Sophie tonight. Maybe they can advise us."

"Don't worry, Peter," Max said in the evening, "the Lord has a thousand ways to help of which we do not know anything. You are paying your tithes. Remember that the Bible says that the Lord will pour out His blessings upon us if we return the tithe to Him? Let us kneel and claim this promise.

"Have faith the Lord is going to help you, " Max said after they had prayed. "The Lord will work things out all right."

Helen wondered what would happen. She had faith that the Lord would help, but how?

"I feel impressed to go back to the garage and try to find the driver to whom I gave the check." Peter said the next morning.

"Do you think that he is still there, and that he will give the check back?"

"It's not very likely. He was to leave the same day; but the Lord can work a miracle that I get it back, and then I can try to get the order through someone else." Peter looked confident.

He was all smiles when he came home. "Helen," he said, "The Lord kept His promise! He really performed a miracle! I went to the garage to find the driver. He was there! I asked him about my check and, can you imagine, he told me that his truck had broken down, and he had not been able to get to Maracay! He still had my check and gave it back to me without any objection! I went to another company which was willing to work with us. They told me to pick up my order as soon as the truck came back to town!"

The trucking company kept its word. "I'm so glad that we are paying tithe. The Lord kept His word!" Peter said.

Peter was able to finish the chicken feed and fill his pending orders. Helen was thankful and happy with the thought that they could put their trust in God. They were not alone. The Lord would lead them.

Chapter 14

Tim

The weeks passed swiftly. The little sticks planted against the fence started to take root and form a hedge. The mandarin and avocado trees grew. Carrots, broccoli, sweet potatoes, and other vegetables did well in the warm, moist climate. Helen's days were full of work. She helped Peter, taking care of the chickens, making chicken feed, working in the yard. Peter was gone part of the time with his panel truck, but Helen did not feel lonely. She had her little girl, nice neighbors, and Gertrud to go on walks with her.

Helen did not feel the emptiness any more. How much their life had changed! They had friends. There was purpose in life. It had meaning!

Her joy was complete when Tim was born the following February. Now she had a little boy again! Now they were a complete family, and she had the hope of seeing her firstborn again when Jesus comes! There was only one worry. Their income did not grow to meet the growing needs of the family.

Max and Sophie continued to visit and help with counsel. One day Max told Peter about a fair coming up. Peter entered his chicken feed and a couple of large beautiful Red Island roosters as handsome as the first one they had bought. Peter got a diploma for his feed and also for the magnificent roosters, but that did not increase their business very much. It was still hard to make ends meet.

"Peter," Helen said one day, "what would you think if I'd try to sell books as Max does? I can speak enough Spanish now. I think I can do it. I think it will bring more income than the sale of *El Centinela.*"

"But what about Helga and Tim?"

"You can take care of them for a few hours some afternoons when you work in the garden. I shall leave right after nursing Tim, and have time enough until he has to be fed again."

She walked fifteen minutes to the bus stop in Chacao, then took the bus to town. The ride took about twenty minutes. She had some success selling books, in spite of having only little time for it. She sold mainly *El Consejero Medico,* a medical book, and some smaller books. One of her favorites was *El Camino a Cristo* (Steps to Christ), by Ellen G. White.

Their income was just adequate with this increase. But it was not long before something happened that made her give up these ventures.

Tim grew to be a nice little boy with such a good disposition. He made funny little noises when he woke up in the morning. Helen kept her resolve to nurse him as long as possible. But nursing was difficult. A neighbor told her to eat toasted sesame seeds. Helen followed her counsel and gained weight. She could not fit into her yellow dress any more. Her doctor was no help. But nursing the baby was more important for her than her weight problem.

Tim was a sturdy little fellow. When he was nine months old he walked around his playpen, holding on to the rim for dear life. His skin felt smooth and good: "sabroso," the neighbor lady said. It felt cool even in hot weather and there was a lot of that lately.

One day was especially hot and oppressive. The sun seemed like a red fireball in a blazing sky. The children played in the living room with Tim's blocks. Helen sewed on her new dress as she watched over them. She remembered that Tim was the same age as Dieter when he died, a week less than eleven months. She thought that she would now see how a little fellow developed further.

Helen looked up at the playing tots. But Tim was not playing! He was not doing anything, just sitting there on the tile floor, his blond tousled head leaning against the wall. His face looked flushed.

Helen jumped up. "Tim, what's the matter, are you sick?"

She swept the baby up and pressed her lips against his forehead. She felt needle pricks of heat on her lips. Tim was ill! He was running a high fever!

"Oh, no, Lord, don't let Tim get sick," Helen prayed. Her fingers trembled as she searched the drawer for the thermometer. It raced up to almost 104°. Panic drowned her thoughts. Tim was seriously ill and at the same age as their first baby when he died—exactly the same age,—one week less than eleven months!

Helen pulled the mosquito net aside and put Tim into his crib. He did not even protest. She took Helga's hand and raced with her to the neighbors to call the doctor.

The doctor tried to calm her. "Babies run a temperature easily. There is no reason to be alarmed. I'm sure it cannot be anything serious."

It was another doctor, not the same they had had three years ago. He could not understand her panic. But he promised to come right away.

"Now, how is our little man? I'm sure there's no reason to be so upset." He tried to calm Helen. She was much too agitated to explain the reason for her fears.

"Let's take his temperature again," the doctor said.

Now it raced to almost 105°.

"Doctor, he's turning blue!" Helen screamed.

The doctor held Tim in his arms. "Fill his bathtub with lukewarm water."

Her whole body shook as she followed his orders. This was a nightmare! This same thing had happened before! Exactly the same thing, and then some hours later her baby would be dead.

"Oh, no, dear Lord," Helen prayed silently again. "Please, please let it not happen again!" But she could not control the chattering of her teeth.

"Señora, there is really no reason to be distressed." The doctor shook his head as he looked at her.

The doctor handed the baby back to Helen. She took the wet clothing off and wrapped him in a towel. The doctor gave him some medicine, and she put little Tim into his crib.

"I'm going to call the pharmacy and have them send the medicine. It should keep the fever down. I cannot make the diagnosis yet, but I'm sure there is no danger. You really don't have to be so upset."

As from far away the words re-echoed in her ears: "Tonsillitis without complications."

Tim looked better, but when Helen tried to give him a drink and his medicine, be turned his face away. Helen told Peter what had happened in the afternoon, and together they cared for the baby.

But as evening drew on, it was apparent that the child was not improving. Tim seemed to grow worse. Helen gave Helga her supper and put her to bed in the big bedroom. She turned on the lamp on the dresser in the children's room. She saw his eyes closed, harsh lines forming in his little face as she bent over the baby. He seemed hewn out of stone, and he felt so hot! The temperature did not drop as the doctor had predicted. Suddenly some jerking movements seized the little boy.

"Peter, oh, Peter, come quickly! Tim has convulsions!" Helen cried.

They stood helplessly by. They did not know what to do. At last the baby was quiet again, barely breathing.

"Let's call the doctor," Peter said.

Peter left to make the call. The frown on his face told Helen that he had not been successful in reaching him.

"The doctor is gone to the movies, they said, and is not expected home early. There is no way to contact him."

It was no use trying to call a strange doctor. Even if they found one who was willing to come at this time of night, he would not be able to find the house. The streets where they lived did not even have names posted.

"Let us call Elder Sherman," Peter said after a while. "The Bible says to call the elders if somebody is ill. Nobody else can help us."

"Pastor Sherman said they will come right away," Peter sounded hopeful when he came back from the telephone.

The minutes passed slowly until the pastor and Mrs. Sherman arrived. They looked into the crib and said, "Your little Tim doesn't seem to be so terribly sick."

Just then the convulsions seized the baby again. Mrs. Sherman gave Tim the lukewarm bath. She seemed to know a lot about treating patients. Her quiet strength felt like a balm on Helen's soul. After the bath, Helen dressed the baby again. His skin felt cooler. She gave him the medicine and put him back into his crib.

"We don't know if the Lord will answer the prayer as we want it, when we pray for Tim," said Pastor Sherman. "We don't know what He deems best. We have to pray that His will be done. We have to trust Him. But before we pray, if there is anything to be righted between you two, do it now. Confess to each other any wrongs you might have committed. Then I will anoint Tim, and we will pray for him."

This they did. They tried to remember any wrongs since the beginning of their marriage and asked each other's forgiveness. If only Tim would get better, nothing else mattered. Then they knelt beside the crib as Pastor Sherman anointed Tim's forehead and offered prayer. Helen felt a great calm come over her. She trusted the Lord. Tim's destiny was in His hands.

The pastor opened his Bible to Romans, chapter 8, verse 28, and read, "And we know that all things work together for good to them that love God, to them who are the called according to his purpose."

He took Helen's hand and said, "Trust in God, that His will be done, and that it will turn out as it is best." Then Pastor and Mrs. Sherman left.

Helen and Peter stayed up with Tim. He did not seem to improve.

"You had better go to bed, Peter." Helen said at last. "You have to work tomorrow. I'll stay up with Tim."

Tim's little face again looked like stone. He was unconscious. Helen knelt and prayed again and again, that God would heal him. She turned the light so that it would barely reach the baby. He looked just like their firstborn during his last night. Fear clutched at her heart again, but then she thought of the verse Pastor Sherman had given them. She read over and over, "All things work together for good for those who love the Lord...."

She loved God with all her heart. She believed that He wanted the best for them. How different was this night from the time when Dieter died. Helen did not have any faith then. There was nothing to hold on to during that shattering experience, and the death of the baby then seemed terribly final, without hope.

Now she had something to hold on to. She could stretch out her hand and find a Friend, somebody to help through this night. She thought again about the verse in the Bible: "All things work together for good for those who love the Lord. " How could it work for good if she would lose this baby too? But the Lord had promised it would. The hours passed slowly, while she pleaded with God.

Helen felt as if her heart was breaking when she prayed at last, "Lord, I love you with all my heart. Let your will be done. If you want to take Tim too, it's all right with me; take him, too."

With tears streaming down her cheeks, she looked up at the window. The darkness was softened by the first faint light as the new day dawned. She looked at Tim. His face was relaxed; his little chest rose rhythmically in healthy slumber. The light increased, and the night gave way to pure joy! God's will had been done, and Tim was getting well!

Chapter 15

Perfect Timing

Tim had passed the crisis and was getting better, but he developed a rash over a good part of his body. The doctor came and shook his head.

"This is the tenth case in my fifteen years of practice." He shrugged his shoulders. "I do not know what it is."

The rash cleared up after a few days, and Tim developed several boils on his head. But at last he got well.

Then the chickens developed cannibalism, pecking at one another. The egg production went down.

"I don't know what to do about the chickens," Peter said. "I asked Max, and he does not know either. Guess we'll have to kill and sell them."

Helen suffered a physical breakdown. The strain had been too much in spite of her trust in God. She could not digest her food, not even oatmeal. It got better after her doctor prescribed hydrochloric acid, and the Lord provided help. Mrs. Sherman invited her to stay with them until she got some of her strength back. Mrs. Simon, their lawyer's wife, offered to take care of Tim, and Helga stayed home with Peter.

Now Helen had time to read some of the books from Ellen G. White. Helen was impressed with their insight and wisdom. She gave counsels on health and many other subjects. At a time when physicians prescribed smoking for asthma, Mrs. White wrote that it poisoned the body and should be discarded. In the book *Testimonies for the Church,* Volume 2, written in the years between 1868 and 1871, she had already written about electrical currents in the nervous system. Ellen White became Helen's favorite author.

Mrs. Sherman gave Helen vitamin B shots every day, and she improved with the good care and nourishing vegetarian meals. Helen got some of her strength back after a few weeks of rest, and went home to take up again the responsibility for the family. But she was not strong enough to continue selling the books and the *Centinela* magazines.

Peter's health had suffered too. His leg became badly infected from scratching a mosquito bite. Red lines went up his leg.

"It's blood poisoning," the doctor said. "You should stay in bed for the next few days."

It took quite a while before his leg got better. He could not drive his panel truck to the factories and ball games. They prayed and asked the Lord to help.

"Helen," Peter said, "we have to do something to get our health back. A change of climate would be good for us. I think the best would be if we take a vacation, sell the panel truck and get a car so that we can drive to a better climate where it is not so warm and humid."

"But where would we go, and how can we afford to take a vacation?"

"Someone told me about La Mesa de Esnujaque some time ago. It is high up in the Andes. There is supposed to be a little hotel, run by some German people. It's supposed to be very reasonable in price. We still have some wallets, sewing kits, and other small things from the store. Hopefully we can sell them there to pay for our stay in the hotel."

"But you are supposed to stay in bed."

"I know. You can go to town. You know where Mr. Reyes' garage is. He's the one who sold me the truck. I know him quite well. He may trade it in for a good used car."

Helen took the bus to town. There were about six or seven cars in Mr. Reyes garage. The prettiest was a dark grey one, with not too many miles on its speedometer. It drove all right too. She was proud of her choice.

Mr. Reyes drove her home. He agreed to take the panel truck in payment. He did not linger long, got into the truck and left.

"Helen!" Peter cried after inspecting the car a little closer. "Did you look at the tires? They are all recut! They were originally smooth, and someone cut some designs in them to make them look as if they still have tread on them! That's worse than bald tires! We cannot go anywhere with these tires!"

After a few more days Peter was able to drive to town and trade the car in against a green Ford. It did not look as good as the grey one, but had more tread on the tires. Soon Peter improved enough to be able to make the trip.

It was a long drive. The road led through meadows in the plains after passing the mountains around Caracas. Cows and horses grazed in the green fields. Helga looked at them with wide-open eyes, her little face beaming with happiness.

Tim cried, "Vaca, vaca!" stretching his little arm and hand as far as he could to point at the cows, and "Burro-carrallo," "burro-carrallo," rolling his R's like a native Venezuelan. He could not distinguish between donkey (burro) and horse (caballo).

The road led through the middle of a large creek bed with high banks on each side. Friends had told them before the beginning of their journey to inquire at the little huts at the side of the road if it was safe to drive through. Sometimes rain in the mountains came with such suddenness and force it swept away cars with unwary people who had not taken that precaution. Fortunately it was dry, and it did not rain in the mountains.

They drove along a wide river. The verdant mountains at the sides got higher and more picturesque. At last they came to the needle curves leading up to la Mesa de Esnujaque.

The little town nestled between high mountains close to the Paramount, the highest peak of the Andes. Small, mud-walled houses lined both sides of the narrow, treeless streets. The little hotel was just what they had been told. It was a one-story building, with the large patio serving as dining-room. Tables were set under the wide eaves surrounding it. The guest rooms located across the street were small, painted white, with the usual lone bulb dangling on a long cord. The windows had no glass or screens; only wooden shutters.

A German lady was their hostess. She even prepared real German dishes, creamed turnips, and filled cabbage! She agreed to take some of the samples they had brought for payment.

Helen enjoyed her stay in the fresh, cool air of the mountains. It did not take long before she felt stronger. She did not worry about what to do when they went back. She trusted the Lord. He would provide some opportunity to earn money. Helen went with Peter and the children on walks through the little village and met a German family living nearby. They invited them for tea.

"I have been a member of the Nazi Party." Their host told them. "I'm glad they did not put us into concentration camps. The only restriction is that we cannot leave town."

How thankful Helen was, that they had not been involved in politics! They were able to travel freely.

Coming back from one of their walks, they were greeted by their hostess holding out an envelope to Peter.

"A telegram came for you."

Peter reached for it and tore open the envelope. "Oh!" he said. Helen saw his eyes lighting up.

"It's from Dr. Simon!" he shouted, "Helen, we have been taken off the Black List! Thank the Lord! And just in time! It could not have been more perfect!"

They returned home. Peter wrote to his firms in Canada, the United States, and South America. They had kept their promise to wait until Peter was taken off the proclaimed list. Soon the offers and samples arrived. Peter rented a small office in town and started to build up his business again. The Lord blessed him. Business was good. After a short time Peter was able to hire several salesmen, a bookkeeper, and an office girl.

Chapter 16

Doris

The year 1944 came to an end. The terrible World War II was raging. How thankful Helen was that God had led them out of Germany to Venezuela, far away from the horrors of the war, and they had been able to provide help for their families and friends when the need was greatest. How much Helen looked forward to a time when there would not be any more wars, no more suffering, pain and death, and the people would live together peaceably.

During the war years correspondence with their families was scarce. Helen and Peter prayed for their families in Germany and England. It was at the end of 1944, when Peter came home with a letter in his hand.

"A letter from your brother, Fritz." Peter held it out to Helen. "And it's from New York!"

Helen read that Fritz was now at a camp for prisoners of war, close to New York. He had been in Russia and had caught the last train to the West. He had arrived in Hamburg, was captured by the Americans, and within one week had gotten from Russia to New York.

He wrote that, as far as he knew, Helen's father, and Peter's parents were all right. Helen was happy and thankful that her brother and loved ones were safe. She was thankful for God's help and guidance, and their many blessings.

The children were healthy, growing fast. "We really don't need a den." Helen said one day. "It would be nice if Helga could have her own room. We could fix the den up for Tim. Then each of the children could have a room."

She painted the ceiling. It might have been her stretching out so far, or perhaps it was the fumes of the paint, but Helen had a miscarriage a few days later. The doctor said that she had been pregnant, but that the baby had died and was infecting her. She probably would not be able to have more children.

No more children, ever? Helen trusted God, but there was still a nagging fear: what if anything would happen to one of the children? She would have only one child! The thought tormented her. She wanted another baby.

The war in Europe ended in 1945, and it was in August that the doctor proved to be wrong, when Doris was born. Helga was almost four years old and Tim about two and a half.

Doris was a good baby; never cried, just smiled when Helen looked into her crib in the morning. But she was too good. Because she did not cry, she did not develop her lungs. She had bronchitis every month and frequent asthma attacks. Wrestling for breath, her little face turned blue.

At the end of 1945 a letter arrived from Hamburg, announcing the passing of Peter's dad. They were sad that they had never seen him again after leaving Germany. There were now only Peter's mother and Helen's father left in the old country. But their consolation was that they had the means to let his mother come to live with them. Peter made arrangements for his mother to join them.

They looked forward to her coming, but there were other problems. Doris' bronchitis developed into pneumonia when she was seven months old.

"Fortunately we have a brand-new medication," the doctor said. "It is supposed to be very effective. It is called penicillin. You have to give the baby a shot every three hours through the day and every four hours through the night."

Helen had never given shots. She cringed when the doctor showed her where to put the needle, but did as she was told. During the night Peter gave the shots. The baby cried and hardly went back to sleep, before the next shot was due, but she got well after a few days.

Doris continued to have asthma attacks. She ran a high fever when she was fifteen months old.

"The baby has something wrong with her intestines," the doctor said. "Don't give her any liquids to drink."

After dinner in the evening Helen took Doris' temperature. It shot up to almost 105°. Helen stared at it and called Peter.

"I can't imagine, Peter," she said, "that Doris shouldn't drink any water. She is so hot. She needs liquids. Help me to give her a lukewarm enema."

As they cared for the baby, Helen heard some rattling of dishes in the background, but she was too busy to pay much attention.

Doris seemed to have absorbed all the water from the enema. She felt less hot and soon fell asleep.

Helen went to the kitchen. What she saw touched her heart. There was little Helga, only five years old, standing on a chair pulled up to the sink, washing the supper dishes!

Another doctor was called the next day. He came early in the morning.

"Give the baby lots of water to drink," he said. "The child has tonsillitis, and needs to drink lots of liquids."

"What shall we do about the asthma attacks?" Helen asked.

"Your baby might be allergic to something," he said. "I'll tell you what has helped in many of my cases. Give her three drops of lemon juice, increasing them by three drops every three days, until she gets a whole tablespoon full; then go back to the three drops a day. Give her no canned baby food, only fresh pureed food."

Doris was still very ill through the next days. Helen kept watch through the nights. There was not much time for Helen to sleep during the day. Peter left early in the morning and came back late, and she had to take care of the children. One day Helen felt especially tired. She lay on her bed. Helga came in and sat beside her.

"Mommy," she said, "when I'm grown up you don't have to work so much anymore. I'll help you." Precious little girl!

Doris improved. Helen did not know why. Was it the lemon juice or the fresh food? But whatever it was, Doris did not have any more asthma attacks.

At the beginning of 1947, when Doris was almost one and a half years old, Peter's mother was able to join her family in Venezuela. At last the day came when she arrived. Peter drove to Maiquetia to pick her up. She was short and thin, looking more fragile than Helen remembered her. Her hair had become a little whiter, and the suffering from the war was etched into her wrinkled face. Helen was glad to have her with them.

With all this going on, Helen did not see her friend, Gertrud, for a few months. Word came that her husband had had a heart attack. Helen hurried over to Gertrud's house. She knocked on the door and Gertrud's maid opened.

"Oh, señora, did you hear it?" She wailed.

Helen's heart shrank in her. Gertrud's and the little girls' tear-stained faces told her the bad news.

"Oh, Helen," Gertrud sobbed. "Carlo passed away. He died three days ago. The funeral was the day before yesterday.

"No! What happened?"

"The hospital called that he had had a heart attack. The nurse turned around on the way to his room and said, 'You know, of course, that your husband is dead?' Just like that. Can you imagine! 'You know, of course, that your husband is dead?' I didn't know. I didn't expect it." Gertrud kept shaking her head, tears rolling down her cheeks.

Helen felt stunned. How could she help Gertrud? She felt so inadequate. She knew that her friend was not interested in religion. Gertrud, too, had grown up in Germany and had the same kind of teachers Helen used to have.

"What am I going to do?" Gertrud wailed, "I don't know anything about our business. How am I supposed to support us?"

Helen was sad that she had no answer. She felt bad not being a better witness.

Gertrud sold her house and moved into town. They lost contact, and Helen later heard that Gertrud married one of her husband's salesmen. She also heard that life expectancy for men was only fifty years. Gertrud's husband was not yet fifty years old when be passed away.

Helen thought of Peter. He was now thirty-six years old. Would there be only fourteen more years for him? The children would not be on their own by then.

The work at the office was a heavy load for Peter. Grandma made the suggestion that Helen should help him at the office and employ a housekeeper. Many displaced people were coming from Europe. It would be easy to get help.

Peter and Helen got acquainted with a young couple from Poland. They were looking for a job, and Peter and Helen employed them to take care of the children and the chores at home. The young Polish couple was conscientious and reliable. Helen trusted them with the children, especially because Grandma was there too. The children were not alone with complete strangers.

Only two blocks from their home was a Montessori Kindergarten. There was no problem in enrolling Helga, and they also accepted three-year-old Tim when Helen explained their circumstances. Later both children went to the little private Catholic school close by.

"Mommy," Helga said one day, "I don't know what to do. In school the teacher prays to the Virgin Mary. She wants Tim and me to pray too."

"Just tell the teacher that you pray to God in the name of Jesus, and be real quiet when the others pray."

"The teacher said that it would be all right just to be quiet," was the report she got the next day.

Helen was happy that her little girl had taken her stand for her belief. But, oh, how she wished she could stay home with the children! She left with Peter early in the morning. They came home about eight o'clock in the evening to a late supper, when the children were in bed. The only day they had time with them was the Sabbath.

"Peter," Helen said one day, "I don't like the way things are going. I don't like to be away from the children during the whole day."

"I know." Peter shook his head. "And the climate is not good for Doris either. Besides, I don't have much confidence in the doctors here."

"And, Peter, I don't like the fact that our church school is too far for the children to attend, and that we don't have a high school here in Venezuela. Remember the parents on the *Klaus Horn* and Consul Weber? They brought their children to Germany to attend school."

"Yes," he said, "and many of the Venezuelans who can afford it send their children to the United States to attend high school. From our church they send the children to Medellin, Columbia."

"The Vitos are sending their children to Berrien Springs. They cannot even come home for vacations, because the trip is too expensive. I would not like that." Helen shook her head.

"I don't want to send the children away when they are only fourteen years old." Peter said. His eyes looked troubled. "Would it be better to go to another country, make another new start as long as we are still young enough?"

"But where would we go? What would we do?"

"Maybe we can go to the United States. Maybe I can get a job in the export business there," Peter said. "At least we may find a better climate and better medical help and schools."

"Yes, and I could be at home with the children and Grandma, and maybe we can locate near some woods. Oh, how much I would like to walk in the woods again!"

"All right," Peter said. "Let's make a trip to the United States, to see how we like it there and where we would like to settle."

"And, Peter, we can visit my cousins in Texas and my relatives in New York."

"First we'll have to see if we can get passports. Remember the German people in The Mesa de Esnujaque could not even leave their little village," Peter said. "There is no German embassy here where we could get a passport. We'll have to see if we can get one from the Venezuelan government."

Chapter 17

U.S.A.

Because they had not been politically active, Peter did not have any problems getting their emergency passports from the Venezuelan government. He went to the American embassy and got their visas allowing them travel to the United States.

Despite her anticipation to see her relatives it was not easy for Helen to leave the children, but she trusted that God would lead them to a place where it would be better for Peter, healthier for Doris, and where she could stay home with the children. They decided first to investigate the living conditions on the east coast. Peter was sure that he would be able to get a job there in his field of import and export.

They took the large propeller plane in Maiquetia. It flew at a much lower altitudes than the jet planes nowadays. They flew through white, fluffy clouds. There was much turbulence at this altitude. The stewardess gave the travelers gum to chew to keep their ears from hurting. The cabins were not well pressurized.

Helen enjoyed the trip and seeing her relatives, but she was disappointed. It was hot and humid on the east coast.

"Peter," she said, "It seems that it is almost just as moist here as in Caracas. I am concerned that the climate would not be good for Doris. The children don't look very healthy either. I don't think we should move here. What do you think?" she asked.

"I thought so, too," he answered. "Maybe we can make another trip next year. But I do think we should move to America. We should at least apply for an immigration visa."

How glad Helen was to see the children when she got home! The young couple had taken good care of them and Grandma. But the young husband had been able to get employment more suited for their needs.

Peter hired a young girl to take care of the children and tall, dark-blond Elsie as housekeeper. Elsie spoke German. Her blue eyes sparkled and she looked strong and healthy. She had just come with her fiance from Latvia. Elsie went to church with the family and after church went to visit with her fiancé. It was not long before Elsie asked Helen to study the Bible with her.

Elsie devoured her lesson just as Peter and Helen had done, and after a few months she was ready for baptism.

But there was a problem for Elsie. Her fiancé did not approve of her becoming a member of the Seventh-day Adventist church. She had a real struggle to decide between her love for him and her love for Jesus. At last she decided for Jesus, and Helen had the joy of seeing Elsie being baptized. Her fiancé kept his word and broke off with her.

That did not daunt Elsie. She was on fire for the Lord. She wanted to dedicate her life to bringing the message to others. She quit her job and started canvassing, selling the books Helen used to sell and loved so much.

Peter hired another housekeeper, Mrs. Eggers, an older Christian lady from Estonia. She looked neat and clean, with her brown hair put up in a bun at her neck, her grey eyes exuding kindness. Helen felt at ease with her. She felt she could trust Grandma and the children with her and the young girl during their absence.

Peter and Helen decided to make their trip to the west coast during the next spring. In the meantime Peter applied for an immigration visa at the U.S.A. embassy.

"Helen," Peter said when he came home "they told me at the embassy that we should make up our minds and not drag the decision out too long. Soon many people are expected to come from the European countries, and there will be a long waiting list to immigrate to America."

In late spring of 1948 they took the trip to the West Coast. It was on a Friday when they got to San Jose, situated not far from San Francisco. Sheltered by the low mountains of the Santa Clara valley, it had a better climate than the larger city. It was warmer and not so windy. Peter and Helen checked into a motel and went to church the next day. They got acquainted with some members of the church. In the afternoon they drove around.

"What to you think of San Jose?" Peter asked when they came back to their room. "The town is not very large, only about 50,000 people. The climate it good. We are not very far from San Francisco. Maybe I can get a job at an export house here."

"And I like how the children look. They look so good with their red cheeks." Helen smiled. "I like it here. Our church has an eighth grade school in town, and an academy in Mountain View, not very far from here. I heard that the children can commute by train to Mountain View."

"It is not very far from the ocean either." Peter nodded assent. "We can go to the beach. The children would like that."

"You think that we should move here?" Helen asked.

"That's a possibility," was Peter's answer. "I like it here better than at any other place we have seen up to now."

Helen flew home before Peter, who wanted to visit some suppliers in San Francisco. She stopped in Texas, to get acquainted with her cousins in Galveston and Houston. Helen told them about their plans to immigrate. Her cousin John said that they would be happy to be guarantors for them, to facilitate their immigration.

It was not difficult to find a buyer for the house and the business after returning home. They sold their furniture and most of their belongings. They packed only the most necessary things. Each person was allowed 55 lbs. of baggage on the plane.

In January, 1949, the great day arrived. For the last time the family drove the hairpin curves down to the coast. It was hot in Maiquetia at the airport, but they shivered when they arrived at New Orleans around midnight. It was cold! The next morning they made a beeline to the closest department store to get winter clothing for the children.

Peter bought a used Buick to continue their travels, but Grandma was not strong enough to travel with the family for several weeks. Peter found a friendly German couple with whom she could stay until they knew where to settle.

Peter drove with the rest of the family to Texas to meet Helen's relatives. Snow had fallen in Texas for the first time in many years. How the children enjoyed playing in it!

They continued traveling toward California. It took four weeks before they arrived in San Jose again. In their travel they did not find another place they liked better. It seemed a perfect place to raise the children.

They found a motel with a little kitchen and sent for Peter's mother. They stayed several weeks in the motel until they found a house they liked in a quiet street in the suburbs.

On the first weekend in their new home, Helga and Tim came down with the measles, and Doris followed suit while Helga and Tim were recuperating. How thankful Helen was that the children did not get sick when they were still in the motel! It was so much easier to take care of them in their own home.

But as much as they liked San Jose, there were no export firms. Peter could not find a job in his line of business. It would have been much easier in San Francisco, but the environment would not have been good for the children; and they remembered the warning in Ellen White's writings not to settle in a large city. Peter continued looking for a job.

It was good to go to church on Sabbath. One day a week they could forget their concerns for the future. They felt confident that God would lead them. They first went to the English church, but then joined the Spanish church. It felt more like home, and the children could only speak Spanish and a little German.

They heard that the church had a camp meeting in Soquel every year. It was about an hour's drive over the mountains toward Santa Cruz at the coast. They heard that one could rent a tent with some bedsteads, but without bedding. There would be a restaurant and also a store as well as some cook-sheds for preparing meals.

"That do you think about going to campmeeting, Helen?" Peter asked. "I don't have a job yet, and ten days will not make much difference."

"Oh, Peter, I'd like that. I heard that they expect some good speakers."

Helga, Tim, and Doris were excited when they heard the news. A few days later the family took off with Grandma and the children, the car loaded full with bedding, clothes, kitchen utensils, and all they would need during the ten days of the meetings.

Campmeeting was a delight. The children went to their own meetings in the children's tents. Helen went with Peter to the Spanish tent.

"Helen," Peter said a few days later, "I heard that there is also a German tent here. Let's go to that one today."

"You mean there are meetings in German?"

"Yes, and they are supposed to have good speakers too. So, let's go."

Helen was surprised to see so many people when they got to the tent. The first song in German she heard since her church visits as a child was "God is love." It touched her heart. Germany had become unreal in her mind, a distant memory. Too many things had happened, too many moves from country to country, even changing their language a few times. Germany had been like a long-forgotten dream. But this was real. They did come from Germany, and even German people believed in God! It seemed as if a large circle had been closed. It felt like coming home, and there would always be someone to hold her hand. Helen was overwhelmed. Tears streamed down her face.

Coming back to San Jose, Peter continued looking for a job. But as much as he tried, he could not find anything in his line of work.

"The only job I can get is washing boxes at a packing house," Peter announced one day. "It's better than nothing, but we have to have more income. We cannot send the children to church school with what I am making. We do want to stay here in San Jose. They have a good church school here."

"I know." Helen shook her head. "I know we have to start something different. But what can we do?"

"Remember how the Lord had guided us to solve our problem when we came to Venezuela?" Peter asked. "At that time we thought either to produce something people would use or provide a needed service."

"And at that time I did not even believe in God. I know he will lead us to find something. But what?" Helen asked.

Chapter 18

San Jose

Helen thought about their start in Venezuela. At that time, even if she did not pray, God had led them all along. There had been many problems, but always He had helped them to find a way out of their difficulties. She was confident that God would find the right solution for them once more.

"Peter, I think I should start canvassing again," Helen said one day. "Helga and Tim are going to school, and we could bring Doris to one of our church members. It would not be very expensive. She has a little boy Doris' age with whom Doris can play. But we should live close to the school so that the children could walk home."

They sold their house in the suburbs and moved into a smaller one on East Santa Clara Street. But Grandma needed more care which Helen, being absent most of the day, could not provide. Peter again found a pleasant German couple to care for her.

Helen was delighted to find out that she did not have to start canvassing cold turkey as she had done in Caracas. Someone from the publishing department of the church went with her for a few days. They went to the predominantly Spanish-speaking section of San Jose. Helen sold the big medical book *El Consejero Medico* and some small books, El *Camino a Christo* (Steps to Christ) and *Por Sendas Extraviadas (The* Marked Bible). Helen did all right, but she did not like to be gone from home so much. Besides Peter needed another kind of job and might need her help.

Maybe they could build up something together. The beautiful display of watches at the little store in Santo Domingo came to her mind.

"How about a watch-repair business?" Helen asked one day.

"A watch repair-business?" Peter frowned. "I know about watches, but I'm not a watchmaker."

"We can learn, don't you think so?" Helen queried.

"But you know that my eyes are not good enough," Peter said.

"But mine are good. I can get instruction in watch repairs."

"Then I could build up the wholesale business in the meantime. I could contact some watch importers in New York and sell to the stores."

Peter found the addresses he was looking for in the telephone book. It took only a few days before he received the offers. He ordered a supply of Swiss waterproof watches and soon was ready to travel to find some customers.

Helen found a retired teacher from the college who took a couple of students to teach watchmaking, not just repairing! He taught Helen to temper, cut and polish small steel rods to make her own tools. She learned to make her own little drills and the tiniest screws, even cut her own staffs. The staffs had two mirror-polished pivots and two shoulders, one with an undercut for the hairspring, one for the roller jewel. The tiniest ones for lady's watches were scarcely an eighth of an inch long.

Then the teacher showed her how to repair watches. It took about a year and a half, without vacations, until she was ready to start their own business.

They sold the house and found one for sale a few blocks further down on the other side of the street. It seemed to be a better location for a watch shop and had space enough to build a store in front. They had to take a substantial loan to have the store built.

The front of the store had some showcases with white wood frames, looking like picture frames, and a recessed entry with a three-sided showcase. The entrance door was of heavy glass. A door from the store to the little hallway gave Helen easy access to the house.

They bought some giftware and other merchandise from New York, and because they imported music boxes and watches from Switzerland they called their store *The Swiss Shop.*

Peter had a sign printed on the door of the store: "Closed from Friday sundown to Saturday sundown."

"You will never be able to make a living if you have the store closed on Saturday," an acquaintance told them.

"I don't think it will hurt us to keep God's commandments and have the store closed on Sabbath," Peter answered. "I think He will help and bless us."

Peter was right, the Catholic church, just a few blocks from the new store, was on the same side of the street. The location was perfect. The store was open on Sunday mornings. On the way to church the people brought in their repairs or did their buying.

But it was a struggle to make ends meet. Helen did not have time to sew any more. She bought the girls dresses at the Kress department store. The dresses cost $ 2.95 and $ 3.95. The ones for $ 3.95 were so much prettier, but Helen and Peter needed the extra dollar to make the payment for the next promissory note when it became due. But they always made it. Sometimes in the nick of time.

Peter traveled a great deal. Helen tended the store and repaired watches, sometimes until after midnight. It was not exactly what she had dreamed of when she first thought of moving to the States, but at least she was not too far from the children.

Helga, now about nine years old, must have remembered the promise given when Helen had been so tired. She cleaned the house on Fridays, getting Tim and Doris to help. She helped with the cooking when she was a little older, and even baked a cake for Sabbath! Once she saved up from her little allowance to buy some pretty dark-brown material with little red roses to make a dress for Helen, and Tim saved up to buy a blouse and for Christmas even a dress for his mother.

It was always difficult to raise the tuition, but it never occurred to Peter and Helen to send the children to public school. Helen knew too well what damage that could do, and Peter agreed with her.

The teacher from school had asked Helen to talk English with the children to enable them to learn the language faster. It had not taken long before Helen noticed that the children were speaking English with each other at home.

"Peter," Helen said, "Helga and Tim would like to go to the English church, because most of their friends are there. I like our Spanish church. What do you think we should do?"

"We have good friends in our church, but I realize that the children might be happier in the other one. It's all right with me if we change."

They changed their membership and met new friends. A couple of them, the parents of one of Helga's friends, lived only a short distance away. The father was traveling a lot and Eva, the mother, was a nurse.

Helen got acquainted with their neighbors, Harry and Jean Smith. Jean's warm smile and the twinkle in her brown eyes made Helen feel drawn to her. Jean became a real blessing for Helen. She hired her to take care of the store when Peter was out of town and Helen had to run errands.

Things seemed to work out all right, but soon Peter and Helen had to face more difficulties. Peter's mother needed more and constant care, which the couple with whom Grandma was living could not provide. Grandma was also homesick for Germany and wanted to go back to her homeland. Peter corresponded with one of his aunts in Germany, and she offered to have Grandma come so she could care of her.

It was a hard decision, but they could not see another solution. Peter took Grandma back to Germany in June 1952. He also visited their suppliers and was gone for several weeks.

Helen missed not being able to attend camp meeting that summer. "Let's drive over to Soquel on Sabbath," she said to the children one Friday. They responded enthusiastically.

They left early in the morning to drive over the hills to Soquel. It was just after lunch when Helen felt her throat becoming sore. She called the children together and started to drive home. Her throat got worse rapidly. She had severe chills, and just managed to drive into the driveway, and call the doctor and her friend Eva.

"Strep throat," the doctor pronounced after checking Helen.

Her fever must have been very high; Helen did not remember much of the night, only that Eva stayed and gave her the medication.

It took several weeks before she felt better. What a blessing the Lord had provided through Jean and Eva. How glad Helen was when Peter came home again and could help to provide for the family.

Time for the next gift show came a few weeks later. Peter exhibited his wares at the shows in San Francisco every year. He stayed in the city during that time. Helen took the train to San Francisco in the morning and back in the afternoon to be home with the children when they came from school. Jean took care of the store during the day.

It had taken a couple of trips in their little Opel Squareback to bring the clocks and giftware to San Francisco. Peter could not bring them back in one trip. At that time they did not know anything about U-Hauls. But Eva had a sister who owned a pickup, and she agreed to pick Helen up at the store to bring the clocks and giftware back. Helen had to run an errand before leaving, and Jean came to take care of the store. But as much as Helen hurried, she was a few minutes later than she expected.

"Oh," said Jean. "Your friend was here and I told her you were already gone to San Francisco."

Helen knew that she could not get a train to get to San Francisco in time before the gift show closed. Besides, how would they bring their things home? What could she do? She went into the house to pray. The Lord impressed her to go to Eva's house. She knew Eva was at work. She thought that it did not make any sense to go to her house, but the impression was so strong, she went. At that time people did not yet lock their doors when they left their homes, so Helen went in and called Eva at work to find out if she knew where her sister could be. Eva said that she did not have the slightest idea where she could have gone.

After Helen prayed again, she felt assured that everything would be all right. She left the house and stood at the curb, wondering how calm she was, knowing God would make it all right. But how? Then she saw the pickup rounding the corner!

"I was on my way to Sunnyvale to visit a friend," Eva's sister said. "Jean told me that you were already gone. Suddenly I got the impression to go to my sister's house. I didn't want to because I knew nobody would be home, but I could not drive any further. The impression to turn back was too strong. So I came back and found you standing here!"

Precious Lord! How thankful Helen was for His guidance and help in times of need. Helen was glad that they had made the move to San Jose. Even when it was not quite as she had dreamed. It was so much better than to send the children to another country to school.

Only her dream of walking in the woods had not materialized yet.

Chapter 19

Mountains and Valleys

When Helga and Tim were old enough, they attended summer camp of the church at Wawona, in the Yosemite National Park. When they came home, they told about the good times they had, swimming, hiking, getting instructions in different handicrafts, and sitting around the campfire in the evening singing and listening to the stories.

The smell of pine and bear clover wafted through the air when Helen opened the lid of the washing machine after washing their clothes. Oh, how it revived the memory of her hikes in the woods in Germany! How much she would have liked to get out into nature again! To walk under the trees and smell the fragrance of the woods!

Helen heard that at Wawona was also an Adventure Camp for children too young to attend the regular camp. Counselors were needed when Doris was nine years old, old enough to attend the camp.

"Peter, do you think that I could go to Wawona as counselor? Doris is younger than Helga and Tim when they went for the first time. She does not like to go alone. Do you think that I could go with her?"

"I think that would be all right. Jean can help me with the store. Why don't you apply and see if it will work out?"

It did not take long until Helen got her acceptance as counselor. Soon the day to go to Wawona arrived. Helen felt happy riding with Doris on the bus loaded with nine-year-olds.

Arriving at Yosemite State Park Helen saw stately trees, sugar pines, and sequoias lining the road leading to the valley. Deer grazed on a lush meadow where the bus entered the road leading to the camp. They passed the imposing white building of the Wawona Hotel.

After a short drive they arrived at the camp. A narrow one-story building sheltered the long-stretched-out dining room and a kitchen across from some small rustic, wooden cabins, and a bathhouse. Other cabins lined the road to the camping place, shaded with lofty sugar Pines, surrounded by wooden benches.

How Helen enjoyed the mountains, the trees, smelling the scent of the woods, the bear clover! The ground covered with leaves and pine needles felt soft under her feet. It was like in the forest in Germany. But there was a difference. Then she did not believe in God. Now she believed, and what a difference it made!

A small, rustic cabin was assigned to her where she stayed with Doris and five other little girls. During the day Helen helped teaching handicrafts. In the evening they sat around the campfire, singing and listening to stories. It was all Helen had dreamed of.

Each cabin was in charge of building the campfire for one evening. Not even the fact that Helen's campfire refused to start burning and needed help from other counselors marred her happiness.

Helen's enthusiasm for Wawona was catching. After Helen and Doris came home Peter and Helen decided to go with the children to Wawona every year on Labor day weekend.

But they went only the next Labor day. On a Sunday morning in July the following year Peter got up, sat at the side of the bed and put his hand upon his chest.

"Helen," he said, "I have such a pain here."

"Could it be a heart attack?" Helen queried.

"I don't know. But I really feel bad."

He went back to bed, and Helen called the doctor. It did not take long before he came.

"It's probably nothing serious," he said after he checked him, "but if it gets worse bring Peter to the hospital."

It did get worse. By the time they arrived at the hospital Peter looked grey. He threw up. A cardiologist had Peter admitted and brought him into the emergency room. The smell of antiseptic stirred dreadful memories in Helen's mind. She waited and prayed.

"Your husband has myocardial infarction, a heart attack," was the doctor's diagnosis when he reappeared. "If he makes it through the night, around two in the morning will be the worst time. Then, if he makes it, we can only hope from one day to the other."

He gave Helen some sleeping pills. Helen looked at the pills in her hand. She was stunned. What would happen to Peter? Fear rose in her heart. What would she do if something happened to him?

She remembered the time in Venezuela when Gertrud's husband had died from a heart attack. He, too, had not yet been 50 years old. But then Helen remembered the verse in Romans 8:28 the Pastor had shown them when Tim had been so ill: "All things work for good for those who love the Lord...." She trusted that God would see them through.

She stayed a while in the waiting room, but there was nothing she could do. The children were home alone, and she had to tell them what had happened.

Helen was wide awake around two in the morning. She prayed thinking of the verse in Romans. She listened anxiously for the ring of the telephone; but no call came.

90

During the week, when Helen took care of the store, a song from her hymnal was a great consolation to her.

"When all my labors and trials are over,
And I be there on the beautiful shore,
Just to be near the dear Lord I adore,
Will through the ages be glory for me.

When by the gift of His infinite grace,
I am accorded in Heaven a place,
Just to be there and to look on his face
Will through the ages be glory to me.

Friends will be there I have loved long ago;
Joy like a river around me will flow,
Yet, Just a smile from my Saviour, I know,
Will through the ages be glory to me...."

That song was a real consolation to her. She felt as if she could stretch out her hand. There was somebody to hold on to; and she would see those again she had loved so much. Dieter, and also Sophie and Max. The next day when Helen visited Peter, he had an oxygen tent over his head. On Friday evening Peter was burning with fever. He was very restless.

When visiting hours were over the nurses wanted to send Helen home but she insisted on staying until the cardiologist came and saw Peter. An hour later the doctor arrived and gave Peter a shot. He quieted down and rested more comfortably. Helen went home.

Helen felt the need for reassurance and prayer. She called the retired minister from Aptos, at the coast, who filled in during the time the San Jose church was without a pastor. He told her to kneel while he knelt at his home, and they prayed together over the telephone.

The next day, Sabbath, the church prayed for Peter. That was the turning point! Peter started to recuperate.

Helen was advised by the doctor to prepare vegetarian meals for Peter. He admonished her to strictly adhere to them. He stated that it would help Peter to get well faster and that he might be able to work again in December.

Helen and Peter had become vegetarians after joining the church. But when they engaged a housekeeper, Helen had explained to her about the clean and unclean meats, but did not insist on vegetarian meals. By the time they came to San Jose, they were used to eating meat again. Now that the cardiologist counseled Helen to prepare vegetarian food for Peter, Helen decided to change back to their vegetarian diet for the whole family.

Peter improved so rapidly that he was already able to work at the end of October. He never had any recurrences of his heart problem, even after almost doubling the age of 45 years from the time of the heart attack.

The years passed. The Swiss Shop was sold after Peter built up his wholesale business. The children grew up, got married, and had families of their own. Helen and Peter moved to Northern California, to be close to one of their children.

One day Helen was sitting in their living room. She looked out the window and saw the sun brightening the snowcapped peaks of the mountain range in the distance, filling the California valley with warmth and light. The recent rain had scrubbed the trees and shrubs. The blueness of the sky was dimmed on the horizon.

The storm was over. Welcome rain had refreshed the valley. Sunshine after the rain! Peace and tranquillity after the storm. How much like their lives. Helen wished peace and tranquillity would last forever, but storms will come, and with God's help we will be able to withstand them.

Would she have felt the need of believing if God would not have led them out of Germany, and if they would have stayed with their families? Would she have felt the need of having faith if they had not lost their baby?

How wonderful God had led her! She remembered that a speaker in campmeeting once said, that the baby of a mother who was a Christian would see her baby again when it dies, but if the mother was not a Christian the baby would not be resurrected when Jesus comes.

It was to her as if Dieter had died all over again. She felt her heart breaking. She broke down and cried. She asked the next speaker about it. He said that the Lord knew that she would become a Christian, and that she would see her baby again. Also Ellen White had written that the angels will bring to their mother's arms the babies which had been laid to rest.

That comforted her, but it made her think that she had wanted to go to heaven to see Dieter again. Was it not much more important to see Jesus, her Saviour who died for her? She wanted to see Jesus, even if she would not have her baby back. She looked forward to holding Dieter in her arms again. But still more important was to be with Jesus.

She thought of it how God had led them to so many different countries. She was filled with love and gratitude as she thought of it how the Lord had guided them, even when she was still an atheist.

She looked forward to a time when there would be no more good-bys to good friends and loved ones, no more death, distress and pain. She looked forward to seeing Jesus, living in a better country with a city whose builder and maker is God.